# PRAISE FOR
*This Marriage?*

"Being vulnerable and honest, especially about our marriages, can be a very difficult thing to do. But scripture tells us to share our experiences and learn from one another's testimony. That is exactly what Lizzy and Dave have provided with *This Marriage*. This book gives us the map to a journey of healthy relationships the way our creator intended it. Bravo, Lizzy and Dave!"

—TODD DOWNING, OFFENSIVE COORDINATOR,
TENNESSEE TITANS

"Lizzy and Dave show us through their journey what redemption and grace look like when you're walking in the spirit. They remind us we are all one decision away from changing the course of our lives. So, turn the page: This is your chance to experience the unconditional love of God."

—LESLIE FRASIER,
DEFENSIVE COORDINATOR, BUFFALO BILLS

"Expressions of authentic vulnerability have the extraordinary effect of making the sad and scary parts of ourselves and our relationships not quite so sad and scary anymore. This is the invitation and the gift of Dave and Lizzy's courageous book. By sharing their story, they make it safer for us to do the same, helping us toward the healing that is possible when we own our brokenness and discover that within it exists the raw material of our wholeness and our strength."

—DAVID BERRY, FOUNDER, RULE 31 LEARNING;
VP OF PEOPLE AND CULTURE, MUNICIPAL, CO

"Once I started reading *This Marriage?* I could not put the book down. As a now-70-year-old man (having known Dave and Lizzy for over 20 years), I have come to realize that 'the sacrifices God wants are a broken spirit and a contrite heart.' (Psalm 51:17) This book is about brokenness—the purest form of excellence. Their story of vulnerability will be used to transform marriages. Thanks for your courage and faith!"

—TERRY FRANSON, SENIOR VICE PRESIDENT FOR STUDENT LIFE, AZUSA PACIFIC UNIVERSITY

"Dave and Lizzy Canales bring their two voices together to tell one courageous story of restoration and redemption. The authors understand that we are all storytellers at heart and that when we see ourselves in one another's stories, we realize that we are not alone. Like reading a private journal, this book gives an intimate glimpse into a marriage that had to hit rock bottom to become rock solid."

—MOLLY DAVIS, COACH, NATIONAL SPEAKER, FACILITATOR; AUTHOR OF THE AWARD-WINNING BOOK, *BLUSH: WOMEN & WINE*

"Dave and Lizzy Canales open up with remarkable transparency about the most painful parts of their marriage to show that with Jesus, there is always hope. It is not just that a marriage can be saved, not just that divorce can be avoided, but that God takes the broken pieces and makes something more beautiful than before. *This Marriage?* is the best book on marriage I have ever read, and I will be recommending it to my entire church."

—DR. SCOTT DUDLEY, SENIOR PASTOR, BELLEVUE PRESBYTERIAN CHURCH

"Dave & Lizzy are the epitome of what Jesus imagines married couples should love and live like! The power of Jesus' grace and mercy over their lives is so evident—all the way from their bond to the deeply enriched beauty spiritually of their family and children.

Dave's authenticity and humility are genuinely awe-inspiring not only as a coach for the Seattle Seahawks but, more importantly, as a friend of God! His servitude and compassion is gravitating. His adoration for Lizzy inspires me daily. Lizzy is not only a Proverbs 31 woman of God, but she is an angel on earth. She is an inspiration for women by the way she loves. Their book is a must-read if you want a lasting marriage. Jesus first, always!"

—RUSSELL WILSON, NFL QUARTERBACK


"As we were running wind sprints during the week of our championship game, our head coach continued to ask us a question as he perceived our fatigue: 'How bad do you want it?' By asking us that question, he was saying, 'I know you may feel like giving up, but how badly do you want to win the championship? You may not think you can't do it anymore, but how much does it mean to you? Is it worth it? Are you willing to keep working?' Marriage can have you feeling the same way. As you encounter tough times (which is to be expected), you will ask yourself this question over and over again: is it worth it? This book is a must-read if your answer is 'my marriage is worth it; I'm not going to give up.'

Dave and Lizzy do a great job sharing real-life experiences that should encourage us, warn us, and instruct us. Their marriage serves as an example of what God can do when we say, 'Yes, my marriage is worth it!'"

—**SHERMAN SMITH,** NFL COACH

"The masterpiece, *This Marriage?* is what the culture needs. But, unfortunately, we lack authenticity, and the Canales' give it to us! This book will challenge your marriage's implementation of grace and will offer you and your spouse hope. Dave and Lizzy do a masterful job of being real, raw, and authentic. This is a must-read!"

—**PASTER JONATHAN RAINEY,** NEW LIFE CHURCH

"*This Marriage?* is the one question that changes it all, and throughout the book, I was forced to ask myself the same question. Dave and Lizzy's transparency will lead, guide, and direct you and your spouse to true freedom and authenticity. If you desire to 'connect' or 're-connect' with your spouse, Dave and Lizzy provide the way in *This Marriage.*"

—**SCOTT COOPER,** VICE PRESIDENT,
THE FELLOWSHIP OF CHRISTIAN ATHLETES

"*This Marriage?* takes you on a journey with David and Lizzy as they battle in their marriage toward oneness and a real relationship with Christ. It was gut-wrenching to ride along in their truck and feel the sorrow as their story starts, but it was just as visceral to feel the hope and promise that repentance and forgiveness bring. They are so authentic and courageous in sharing their process with us! You will leave feeling encouraged to start the journey toward a different marriage, one with God in the center. The work is never done, but it is beautiful to be in the midst of the process!"

—**KEVIN AND BEBE NICKERSON,**
LOS ANGELES RAMS CHAPLAIN

# *This*
# Marriage?

*The Question That Changed Everything*

# Dave and Lizzy Canales

MADE FOR
SUCCESS

Made for Success Publishing
P.O. Box 1775 Issaquah, WA 98027
www.MadeForSuccessPublishing.com

Distributed by Made for Success Publishing

First Printing

**Library of Congress Cataloging-in-Publication data**

Canales, Dave and Lizzy
        This Marriage? The Question that Changed Everything
        p. cm.

LCCN: 2018956061

ISBN: 978-1-64146-738-4 *(Paperback)*
ISBN: 978-1-64146-739-1 *(eBook)*
ISBN: 978-1-64146-581-6 *(Audiobook)*

Printed in the United States of America

For further information contact Made for Success Publishing
+14255266480 or email service@madeforsuccess.net

# DEDICATION

To everyone who walked alongside us from the trailhead to the summit.

This book is a dream come true. We came into this process knowing that regardless of how long it took to write it or how many copies we sold, it was all an investment into *this* marriage—our marriage.

We laughed, cried, stomped, and snorted, and we did it all *together*. With each chapter we wrote, it was as if we were going back to marriage counseling. This book gave us the opportunity to address wounds in ourselves and our relationship that never quite healed properly, and it was a gift. Years from now, we will never regret the number of hours we spent together in the best years of our lives.

The gift truly has been the journey, and we can't wait to see what happens next.

# CONTENTS

# FOREWORD

SOMEWHERE, a little over 2,000 years ago, a very wise man was asked his thoughts about marriage, and he replied this way.

"Haven't you read the Scriptures?" They record that God made them male and female from the beginning, explaining why a man leaves his father and mother and is joined to his wife, and the two are united into one. Therefore, since they are no longer two but one, let no one split apart what God has joined together.

That wise man was Jesus, and He was explaining God's perfect plan for marriage. He designed it to be a union that lasts a lifetime and that the husband and the wife enjoy. They are to grow together in a bond that becomes stronger and stronger as time goes on. That bond, in fact, becomes so strong that it can never be broken apart.

That was God's original plan, and that's what every couple envisions when they get married. We proclaim it in our vows. We'll stay together "in good times and in bad times, in sickness and in health, until death do us part ." But more and more in our world today, this is not happening. Instead, we see couple after couple starting with the best intentions but slowly drifting apart until the marriage becomes untenable. Eventually, they split, citing "irreconcilable differences."

If God's plan is for marriage to last a lifetime, and every couple goes into their marriage wanting to make that happen—vowing to make that happen—why are so many marriages failing? And more importantly, what can we do to help us live out our vows and become that "one flesh" that nothing can split apart?

David and Lizzy Canales share some beautiful answers to those questions in *This Marriage?* They started their marriage journey the way so many couples do, with great expectations and a love for each other that was so strong they never dreamed they'd encounter any turbulence. But slowly, problems did come. Distractions crept into their lives, and before they realized it, these two lives, which were supposed to be firmly united, were heading on divergent paths.

However, unlike so many couples today, they didn't let their marriage wither away. They wouldn't let it go. So instead, David and Lizzy resolved to get things back on the right track and rediscover that sense of purpose and that intimacy they had at the beginning.

I'm happy to let you know they have done just that. They have a beautiful family that is thriving in unity, just as God described. The question is, how did they do it? How did they turn *This Marriage?* (one with so many questions) into This Marriage! (one that is a shining example to their children and everyone around them)?

In this book, they share exactly how they did it, with a simple but not easy formula. As you read, you'll see that they had to go back to the fundamental promises they made to each other and the promises they made to the Lord. Then, once they restored that commitment to each other, they allowed God to do His work to turn that question mark into an exclamation point.

I know their motivation for writing this book was to encourage couples and help people find that incredible bond in their marriage that Jesus described. No matter where you are in your marriage journey, this book will help you find the path to becoming—and staying—"one flesh."

—Tony Dungy

# PREFACE

WE NEVER SET OUT TO WRITE A BOOK. Yes, we started sharing our story early, inviting people to witness first-hand our journey out of the dark and into a wholehearted marriage. We only shared when we saw purpose in it, when someone we knew was struggling or for the opportunity for truly authentic connection. We couldn't envision moving forward in our relationships with anything else hidden, despite the potential for the truth to change the dynamic with our people. Many are shocked when we tell them. For some it is incredibly uncomfortable and maybe even convicting. For others, it is like a breath of fresh air and an invitation to go deeper into their own relationships.

Some of the best advice we received was from a fellow traveler on the road to a healed marriage. "The thing is, real leaders aren't the ones with all of the answers; they're the ones willing to go first," he said with a knowing smile, the slightest twinkle of pain mixed with the joy in his eyes. We didn't have to be prepared or ready, trained and tested for the task at hand. We just had to move forward and start telling the truth right then.

This idea is one of the main reasons we decided to write a book about our story in the first place. Our story does not come from years of professional case studies or the discovery of a magical formula that will foolproof your marriage. We are not counselors, nor are we pastors. We cannot give you 12 steps that will prevent you from further failure or running back after your own demons, although if you are looking for a way to stop being addicted to your own comfort, those steps might be a great place to start. We just wanted to go first, to tell a story that is not a "how to" as much as an "us too." We wanted other people to feel safe starting the journey toward a vibrant marriage by helping them see they are not alone.

Writing this book has been like going back to counseling for another round. The act of reliving these events marched us deeper into the valley of our own brokenness, only to find renewed healing and hope through a stronger understanding of what happened. Writing was the necessary and next vital step for the restoration of our marriage.

From the very beginning, we decided not to share our writing with each other until we put together the final manuscript of this book. We wanted to capture our own individual experiences without the influence of each other's memories. Some events one of us remembers more clearly, and a few one or the other outrightly cannot recall. Trauma will do that to you. We intentionally left the two accounts as they were, without trying to make them match up. Over the course of this story, you will see the disconnect between us diminish as we learned to listen and invite each other in. While we will never see or experience things exactly the same, our capacity for empathy and understanding is better than it has ever been.

Just as we have done with our friends around the kitchen table, we offer our heart and soul in our story to give you hope that you, too, can find a way forward to something better.

Welcome to our mess and the beautiful way that God has worked ALL THINGS together for us. We pray that you find yourself somewhere in these pages and have the courage to keep pursuing all that God has in store for you in your marriage and in your heart.

# CHAPTER 1

# THE QUESTION

I KNEW SOMETHING was wrong with our Suburban for a while. But, like most things, until it was an emergency, I was not going to do anything about it. My husband was still in season, working 16-hour days, when it started sounding funny, so I didn't have his help to diagnose the problem. I thought that maybe there was some debris stuck in the wheel or tire, something benign that didn't need time and money to diagnose. Surely, the squeaking sound I was hearing off and on was eventually going to resolve itself, right? After a month or so of rationalizing the strange mousy squeak I heard coming from the driver's side of my car, I finally caved after Dave commented that it was handling funny. When we returned from our annual post-season vacation to Hawaii, I made an appointment to have it checked.

The 15-minute drive to the mechanic was peaceful, the bright winter sun warming my face as we laughed and sang along to the music, still in vacation mode. The mood changed in an instant as I went to hit the brakes, and my foot slammed all the way to the floor. The whole car shuddered as I vice-gripped the steering wheel, willing the car over to the side of the road. Minutes earlier we were hurtling down the freeway and had miraculously pulled onto a quiet side street before that annoying sound became a full-on breakdown.

When I finally had the car pulled into a safe space, I realized time had warped to a standstill. I relaxed my hands, slowly taking a few deep breaths. Time began to move forward again. The car had come to rest within sight of the park we had already planned to play at while the car was in the shop. My entire body was shaking as I unloaded the kids and the stroller, still reeling from how quickly it all happened. Dave drove the final two blocks to the repair shop while I waited at the park. Still trembling, I watched the kids happily racing around the playground, unaware of the miracle that had just occurred for us to walk away unscathed.

An hour later, the mechanic called. "Well, I have good news and bad news. The bad news is, the entire wheel bearing came clean off, and the brake on that side failed as well. The good news is, we can get the repair done today, and you'll be back on the road!"

*Are you kidding me?!* I thought. What if we had been driving down the freeway when that had happened? What would I have done if I had been alone?

Overwhelmed with relief and gratitude, we quickly turned the day into a family adventure. We played at the park, got coffee, and went for a long walk by the creek. The glorious and rare sunny February day felt idyllic considering the circumstances, and we made the most of it. We took it as a chance to be on vacation in our own city. After a delicious dinner at a local pub, we picked up the car, grateful that we were safe and relaxed after a spontaneous family day. It wasn't until we got home that I allowed myself to acknowledge that the wheel was coming off our family, too.

Unloading the kids from the car, exhausted from the roller coaster of a day, Dave jolted me back to reality. "Hey, Jason and I are going to go grab a beer."

The joyride of our post-vacation glow and the relief of a near-catastrophe-turned-unexpected-adventure came to a grinding halt as I stared down the face of how I really felt. Sure, the season was over, and his hours were better for family life, but he was still going to be on his own program when something that felt better or more exciting came along. I was left to take care of *our* home. Alone. Again.

"So, I'm just going to put the kids to bed by myself then?" There was no doubt my cutting tone revealed the anger I felt at yet another night left to manage on my own. He paused, looking at me for an indication of what his next move should be.

"No, it's fine. Just go."

He waited, gauging my reaction and words for their merit. I felt the icy claw of resentment slowly replace the heat of seething anger coursing through my body. Knowing that my feelings had not made a lasting change before, even when I spoke them aloud, I turned on my heels and started the bed-time routine.

It wasn't until later that night, as I lay in bed trying to sleep despite the million thoughts in my head, that I began to process what I was feeling. In my anger, I wanted so badly just to roll over and go to sleep, to somehow make him pay for his decisions with a few days of distance and silence. I had done just that many times before, and although it didn't fix anything, it made me feel better. I knew how to manage my internal chaos with that response. The problem was, I had started the book *The Power of a Praying Wife*, and I couldn't shake what I was learning. I had opened it a few months earlier in my desperation and loneliness over a long away-game week-end. Looking for anything that would fix my silent struggle, I reached again for the book that had been a wedding present but sat collecting dust on our shelf for years.

The very first chapter made it clear that in order to pray for your husband, you have to first start "by praying for his wife." The book is filled with topical prayers to pray for your husband, but I never got to any of those. I kept rereading the first chapter, unable to move on. On those late nights during the season, I had started asking the Lord to show me what I needed to change. Lying in my bed, finding myself in this place once again, I felt the distinct impression that I was not supposed to go to sleep, that I wasn't to retreat to my old way of handling it. Tired and frustrated, I went to the next place of comfort: the fridge.

Staring blankly into the glowing light, I heard the guys talking downstairs. I guess they had decided to stay in for drinks and cigars instead of going out. Curious, I crept to the top of the stairs to listen in. *Were they praying?* Now I was really confused. What was going on? After a few minutes of trying to hear what was being said to no avail, I settled back into bed. Staring up at the ceiling, I waited for whatever it was that I was supposed to be staying up for.

A little while later, my husband lumbered into bed, smelling strongly of cigars and beer. I think he was surprised to see me awake. Normally, I would have gotten into bed and willed myself to sleep so I didn't have to deal with his coming in late. If he felt my resentment, he certainly didn't let on. Instead, he excitedly launched into the cosmic reasons why he had just been promoted to be the new receivers' coach. "How great is it going to be having the players over to our house, you know, to witness our marriage and family, to see how we do it here?"

"What is he talking about?" was all that was going through my head. I was incredulous, the discontent in my heart directly opposing the picture he was painting. I felt stuck and confused, unsure of what the next step was.

And then my heart whispered honestly, revealing what was really going on inside, just as the brake failure on the Suburban had earlier. I waited quietly for a minute, gathering up the courage for what was about to come out of my mouth.

"*This* marriage?" I breathed out. There it was. The truth.

"You don't think so?" he scoffed.

I took a deep breath and willed myself to continue. "I mean, I think we love each other. I think we have fun together. I think we do day-to-day life together day well. But do I think we are living the marriage God intended for us? Not really."

The silence lay heavy in the darkness. I didn't dare move, afraid if I rolled away, we might pretend I hadn't said anything, and the conversation might end.

"Are you happy?" I asked, somewhat bracing myself.

His response was immediate, hitting like a ton of bricks. "No."

It was flat. Truthful. Stark.

My relief was immediate. I wasn't crazy. All this time, I thought that I was the only one feeling this way. I thought that something must have been wrong with me for feeling unsatisfied when so much of our life was good. This? This was new. Acknowledging that we were both profoundly dissatisfied had never happened before.

Nothing more was said after that. I think we both knew something deep in our marriage had shifted. As we drifted off to sleep in the silence, I could feel it. The tiniest spark of hope was kindled, beginning what would eventually turn into a wildfire, burning down the old marriage and bringing forth something entirely new from the ashes.

# CHAPTER 2

# FROM THE BEGINNING

I SPENT MY FIRST YEAR of college chasing after boys and a life of significance. I was constantly on the hunt for "the one." *Ring by spring* is a joke on many Christian college campuses. By the second year, I was tired of competing with other women for attention. I have always been pretty comfortable in my own skin, choosing what I liked instead of whatever was popular around me. After a year of experimenting with significance, I decided I would take some time off from that life. I wore my hair in a messy bun, threw on a tank top with some thrift store gym shorts and flopped around in my favorite worn-in rainbow sandals. My look wasn't exactly screaming "looking for a relationship." I *thought* I was playing it safe and keeping myself off the market.

It was during this time that Dave and I became friends. I had seen him around campus and was happy to look at him from afar. He was definitely easy on the eyes. We didn't become friends until his little brother transferred to Azusa. Where I avoided initiating interaction with Dave, his brother Coba and I instantly fell into an easy, platonic friendship. His wife and I still laugh about how confused people were about the nature of our relationship. On the other hand, Dave was always really nice but never communicated any romantic interest. So, I casually hid my attraction and enjoyed being around him as a bonus to my friendship with Coba.

Dave and I only ever talked around campus, never exchanging phone numbers or anything, so when he graduated and I left for an urban immersion term, I thought that was it. I found myself thinking about him regularly in a way that really bothered me. I had never met anyone I had been attracted to in quite that way, yet I thought he was too good to be true. I felt grossly preoccupied with conversations we had in college and it seemed silly that our interactions still had such a grip on me. We ended up seeing each other a few times, but then I turned my energy to the second half of my degree: I had to spend a semester abroad in Bolivia, doing independent research and working for a nonprofit for my degree in Global Studies. Still, nothing of note had developed and I was willing myself to forget about him.

Living in an unfamiliar city with a Bolivian family who spoke almost no English while wrestling with the painful reality of poverty all around me was taking a toll. I was too busy mentally during the day to think about anything except basic communication and not getting lost, but at night, the loneliness of isolation was suffocating. I craved community. I would reach out to my roommates to hear about how life was just marching on back in L.A. They were working catering jobs, had found a new church, and were spending their free time in the sun at Seal Beach eating breakfast burritos.

This was supposed to be *my* summer! I had arrived in Cochabamba in the middle of South American winter to the harsh reality of high plains, dry and cold, and I had not planned for this. After a few months of struggling through each bewildering day, I reached a breaking point. I was in my room for the evening when it all came to a head. I lay freezing on my floor, despite wearing every layer of clothing I had, and sobbed. I cried until I simply couldn't cry anymore.

Back home, I could go on for a long time without facing these scary feelings. Here in a completely unknown place, where everything about daily living was different and hard, I couldn't ignore the fearful emotions of loss and loneliness. When they finally broke over me, I was consumed with fears about being left behind, being alone forever, and the feeling that I had been running from these fears for a long, long time. Like a dam breaking, my tears released a flood of all-consuming sadness that I had pushed down as deeply as I could for years. Crawling into bed, completely wrung out, I prayed that Jesus would just be with me before I fell asleep.

When I woke up, the cold desperation from the night before was thawing into joy as the sun shone through the window onto my bed. Everything ahead of me looked different in the golden morning light. Even the broken glass bottles cemented to the walls surrounding my house that functioned as a security system had changed from menacing to brilliant jewels in my newly opened eyes. I spent the day in wonder at the amazing experience, a chance to live in a reality so different from my own. I ate at the street-corner salteña stand without fear of getting sick. I rode the crazy local bus, smiling as we weaved dangerously through crowded streets and laughed at my faltering Spanish with my host family at dinner. In place of the fear and loneliness that had been so consuming, a feeling of lightness and excitement changed the way I saw the details of my day.

As I closed my door that night, I felt free. I sat down at my desk and opened my computer to check my email. I literally laughed out loud.

"Hey, girl! I have been trying to get your email for a while now, and I finally tracked it down. How are you doing? What is life like there? I was wondering if you need a ride from the airport when you get back into town? I was hoping we could start spending more time together when you get back?" It was literally everything I could have wanted in an email from Dave staring me back in the face, and on the day after I had relinquished my heart and future to the Lord, no less. Even more astonishing to me was the freedom I felt to just enjoy this surprise correspondence without needing to understand its significance.

For the rest of the time I was in Bolivia, we exchanged emails almost daily, getting to know each other without the confusion of any kind of physical contact. By the time I returned to L.A., we had established a deep, significant friendship. I still didn't know if we would turn that into a romantic relationship, but I was no longer afraid of interacting with him for fear that my secret crush on him would be exposed. Greater than that, I knew that God had a plan that I had not manipulated. Whether or not our relationship ever blossomed into something romantic, our friendship gave me hope for whatever God had in store for my future. Across the equator, something really special was happening, and where dread had been, I now felt excitement for whatever was to come.

———— ❖ ————

Dave: During my junior year at Azusa Pacific University, I went to a basketball game with my roommate Lou. I'll admit, I was semi-interested in the game, but the real reason Lou and I were there was to heckle the opposing team and check out all the girls on campus. It was a ton of fun and provided a much-needed break from writing papers and reading for our classes. As Lou and I were sitting there, panning the crowd, the sound of the referee's whistle reminded me why we were there. It was the first timeout of the game and out came the APU Cougars cheerleading squad.

As football players, we were never able to see the cheerleaders because they lined up behind our bench on the track, facing the stands. But during basketball season, we finally had a chance to see their faces. With an undergraduate population of about 3,500 people, we knew most of the girls on our squad, but I was always interested to see who the new girls were. As the cheerleaders bounced onto the court, my excitement turned to butterflies. To this day, my heart still races when I think about this particular game. One of the girls came trotting out with a longer stride and immediately stood out from the rest. She was a head taller than her teammates, with dark-brown hair and exotic (almost Latino) looking eyes. It felt as if time stopped, and what was supposed to be a 30-second timeout felt like an hour.

It was Lizzy. I was in love.

I couldn't help but notice how amazing Lizzy was. I watched her help lead an on-campus Bible study that we both attended, and I noticed how the other girls always seemed to look to Lizzy when they were going through hard times. Lizzy also organized a few of her friends to make care packages for members of the football team to take with us when we played on the road. And, on a college campus where a lot of the girls dressed for attention, she remained modest. I was falling in love with her—and *hard*.

Unfortunately, the timing of my newfound feelings for Lizzy was horrible. I was graduating from APU in a few months and would be moving home to work, all while she was going to study abroad.

A few months later, I called her to see if she wanted to come with my family and me to Olvera Street in L.A. It is an iconic little alley adorned with all the colors and cultural decorations of a small town in Mexico. Combine that with my big Mexican family, and it was a great test to see how

Lizzy would respond around us. The day I picked her up, I got dressed up, did my hair, put a little cologne on, and drove to the host family's house. I arrived around sunset and waited out front with my cool black Spy shades on, leaning on the hood of my newly washed, cherry-red 1987 BMW. I was laying it on thick. We joined the rest of my family and piled into one of our big white church vans. They were crazy and loud as usual. Lizzy didn't even blink.

*She's perfect.*

After our unofficial date to Olvera Street, we didn't talk or see each other much. The last time we did talk was before she left for Bolivia for the second part of her study abroad term. We said we would keep in touch. However, we didn't. I can't really explain why I didn't reach out, other than wanting to test the strength of my feelings for her and wanting her to have that time without distracting her. After a few months, I decided to reach out so she wouldn't forget about me. I sent an email to her once a week, every Sunday night, for the rest of her time in Bolivia. My last email to her was a week before she was due to return to the U.S. In it, I said, "When you get back, I would like to take you out… alone."

She casually responded, "OK, that sounds great." I think I even offered to pick her up from the airport. I wasn't going to give any other guys a chance to get involved!

The week after she returned, I took her on our first date for sushi at a restaurant called Onami. We had a great time. We talked every night after that, late into the almost morning. We alternated visiting each other in Azusa, where she lived, and in Carson, where I lived with my parents. After one such visit to her apartment, as I was leaving, I stopped in the doorway. I saw her roommate Lisa in the background, and she, sensing that this was a private moment, slipped away into the kitchen. Looking deeply into Lizzy's eyes, I said, "I like you a lot." I felt like Jim Carrey in *Dumb and Dumber*. Even so, she smiled and said, "I like you, too." Then, we had our first kiss.

Over the next nine months, we spent every spare minute we had together. She started coming to our family church, and she came to my first football game as a coach. We were in love. Secretly, I was saving up my pennies for an engagement ring. I had even talked to her sister about the type of ring Lizzy would like. Without her knowing, I took her parents to dinner while they were visiting from Seattle. After some appetizers and small talk, I said, "The real reason I brought you here is to ask you for your daughter's hand in marriage." They chuckled, undoubtedly at the awkwardness of my abrupt shift in our conversation. Bob, Lizzy's dad, looked at me with a big smile on his face and asked, "What took you so long?"

———— ✧ ————

Lizzy: Our engagement will always be a beautiful reminder of the intention we started out with in our relationship. He took me to dinner, and then we went down for a walk on the beach. This was something we had done before, so I didn't think twice about it. I took off goofily, skipping down the beach, and I didn't notice anything different until he pulled me to a stop and turned me to face him. I had a habit of seeing what I wanted to see, not necessarily what was *really* going on. He was serious but happy, and the moment suddenly became high definition as everything else faded into the background. I knew what was about to happen, but I was also completely caught off guard.

"I made you a promise that I wouldn't tell you I loved you until I meant it, and I plan on telling you I love you today and every day for the rest of our lives." He dropped to one knee and pulled out the little box concealed in his pocket. I felt the protective walls I had tried so hard to keep intact around my heart dissolve. All of the angst and waiting did not leave me disappointed. I was going to marry this man! Before I could stop it, deep, joyful laughter erupted from the bottom of my soul as I threw myself into his arms. From here on out, it was going to be he and I together. We didn't have to hold back from each other anymore, and I was so excited.

Later on, I would look back at our early days together and wonder how we had gotten so far off course. I now realize that all our efforts to make this relationship good simply could not cover up the deep wounds we carried and the habitually sinful response we used to deal with these unseen injuries. Our issues were already there, even in the beginning with the simplicity and excitement; we were just good at hiding and pretending. Our love and intention, as pure as they might have been, didn't make those issues go away. Looking back on our dating and engagement during the dark days reminded me that God had brought us together in a beautiful, intentional, and timely way. Maybe somehow, we would be able to feel like that again, to find that purpose together in the future.

# CHAPTER 3

# THE FIVE-YEAR PLAN

AFTER MY SECOND YEAR of being the head coach for the JV football team at my alma mater, Carson High School, Lizzy and I sat down to talk about my career—and our future.

With an apprehensive look as if she was walking out onto thin ice, she said, "Don't take this the wrong way, but you're really good at this coaching thing. You can take this as far as you want to go."

I knew exactly what she meant, and my heart leapt at the thought of it. Excitedly, I said, "Do you really think so? I mean, from what I have heard about the coaching profession, it takes a lot of time away from family."

"I will do whatever it takes to support you and get us there," she said.

The reason she felt the need to qualify her first statement was that she knew what my dream was, and it felt small to her. She could see that I was made for something bigger and that I was holding back. I wanted to be the next head coach at Carson High School and build a "Powerhouse" program. I had also told her of my intention to open a sports performance facility, all while serving faithfully at my dad's church as the worship pastor.

I had it all planned out—or so I thought.

That conversation changed the trajectory of my career, as my wife had given me the green light to take my shot. Being the dreamer that I am, my wheels immediately started turning. This was the beginning of a pattern in our relationship where I offered several dreams to Lizzy and watched her reaction to see if anything stuck. I am the type of person who is living the dream while chasing the next one. Lizzy is the type of person who wants to know what the dream is so that she can start making plans.

After we got married, I continued in both roles, pouring myself out into pursuing my coaching career while simultaneously leading band and worship practices as well as Sunday services. It felt like I was being torn in two. I was struggling with a sense of loyalty and duty to my family, but I was also obligated to this new life my wife and I were trying to create together.

It all came to a head in our second year of marriage. We had spent New Year's Eve splitting time between a party at our friend's house and the church's annual celebration. Based on text messages and voicemails I received, I realized I was expected to be at the whole service. Lizzy and I pulled into the alley entrance of our home, sitting in silence for a moment.

On the drive home, I had been stewing about all the ways I was failing to be a "good son" and contributing member at the church, and I started to unleash my thoughts on Lizzy. It was not until I aggressively said, "If it weren't for you, I would've been there tonight at the church!" that things quickly got ugly.

Lizzy, now fed up, replied, "Is that where you want to be? At the church? Then go!" She stopped me dead in my tracks.

As I was fishing for my next point in the argument, I realized something. She was courageously taking a stand, not to defend herself, but to protect our marriage. I immediately realized the decision that was in front of me.

After a sobering silence that felt like an hour, I simply said, "No."

She knew that I didn't feel called to be at the church long-term, and she wasn't about to allow me to pass the buck of disappointing my family on to her. Then I said, "I want to coach football, and I want to spend more time with you." As you may have noticed, there is a popular theme in this book: a wife who loves her husband so much that she stands up to him and tells him the most difficult truths, regardless of the consequences. Another honest conversation clarifying our vision for our family.

We decided to give ourselves a five-year window to get an entry-level job at a major college. The thought was that if we tried hard to get a break for five years and came up short, we could always fall back on a local job with a lot more expertise.

Three years into our five-year plan, Lizzy and I found ourselves employed by arguably the greatest program in college football at the time—the University of Southern California. While this adventure started off as *our* dream, it was quickly reverting to *my* dream once again… and she was there to help finance it. When we look back at the first five years of my coaching career, Lizzy sees it as her way of investing in our future. She jokingly tells people, "I had to put Dave through medical school." Even though we can laugh about it now, the serious matter is that she had to sacrifice any professional goals she might have had to help me achieve mine.

I was the one going to coaching clinics and conventions. I was the one visiting colleges to meet new coaching staffs and present myself to them. Ultimately, I was the one with my name on the luggage tags and credentials. As I was climbing the American football ladder, I was leaving my wife behind. I guess I always thought that someday, when I became a head coach, I would find a way to get Lizzy involved in what I was doing professionally. What I had failed to realize was that Lizzy's involvement in my job was not contingent upon the growth of my career, but on the growth of our marriage.

———— ✦ ————

Lizzy: I always envisioned my life after graduating would look wildly different than where I found myself in my early 20s. College was a jumble of studying, living off tips from waiting tables, road trips up and down the coast, beach days, and the independence of being unattached. Until I started dating

Dave, I thought I would end up on a beach in Hawaii for a couple of years, working just enough to chase an endless summer. When our lives intertwined, his visions became mine, and I wholeheartedly jumped on board to becoming a coach's wife. Friday night lights replaced sun-soaked beaches, and we fell into step with the beat of a literal marching band.

We had no idea what we were doing, but all that mattered was that we were doing it *together*. Early in our marriage we attended the Coach of the Year banquet at the American Football Coaches Association annual convention. The coach who accepted the award made a speech about how "he couldn't do it without his amazing wife." It was as if I were peering into the future at that moment—I just knew one day I would be sitting at a table watching my husband give that same speech, and I was inspired for the road ahead.

Over time, I began to realize that I was not quite as integral to the world of coaching as I naïvely thought I would be at the beginning. I didn't go on coaching trips with him. Instead of a life of excitement and victory, I was mostly alone while he worked longer and longer hours and chased the next promotion. The dream and the vision remained the same, but in the football world, I was only invited to be a *part* of the dreaming. It was my job to make sure that everything else went off without a hitch. There were no end-of-the-year banquets or speeches. Just the weekly hug down on the field after the game and the 10 minutes I felt important when I got to pick him up at the locker room.

I was learning that my reality would be vastly different than what I had always imagined. Instead of being caught up in a life-changing adventure I was an integral part of, I felt like support staff. I was hungry for something that celebrated me and *my* talents, not just my ability to facilitate *his* dreams. The further up the coaching ladder my husband climbed, the more disconnected and isolated I felt. He was traveling to different cities while his teams played in big stadiums, his network growing with all the pomp and circumstance of the collegiate and NFL football world.

Meanwhile, I was home with a new baby in a new city mostly alone, without the salary I'd imagined would come with all of this as some kind of solace. It was almost as if we lived in two different worlds. The divide between us continued to grow as we learned to stay on our own side and deal separately.

Where I once dreamed of all that could be in the future, I now found myself asking, "Is this really IT? Is this really the life I signed up for?" I would push it away, looking at all the boxes I could check that were supposed to make my life satisfying: healthy kids, handsome husband, success, fitness. But the question was always there, hidden away in a place that I could seldom allow myself to access even in moments of raw honesty. This same question would be the very spark that would ignite our marriage—once I finally allowed myself to say it out loud. For now, it smoldered in deep, secret resentment, widening the growing chasm between us.

"Is this really it?"

# CHAPTER 4

# BALLIN' ON A BUDGET

DAVE AND I never should have been on vacation. We had no business spending a week in Maui (nor did we have the money), but after that first season in the NFL ended, we were desperate for a vacation. We hadn't even gotten our playoff bonus yet, but since we knew it would come while we were away, we went for it. We wanted to pretend our reality was different, even just for a week in the beautiful Hawaiian sun.

Truth is, we were upside down financially. When we were both working, we had enough to comfortably ignore our spending habits and lack of budget. Add in a house and cars we really couldn't afford and then take away my income when I decided to stay home with our new baby, and we were really struggling. Since Dave left his life of teaching and working at the church to coach full time, we had taken a pay cut every year in order to pursue advancement in his career. At this point, with our entry-level salary in the

NFL, we were just below the poverty line for the State of Washington. We were living in debt and barely making ends meet month to month.

After months of insomnia over our deepening financial pit, I finally invited my mom into our troubles. She thoughtfully did some research and connected us to a debt consolidation company that would prove to be a gamechanger for Dave and me. We had to forfeit our credit cards while they managed the repayment of our debts, making sure that we learned how to live only on the cash we brought in. Slowly and ever so surely, we began to see a tiny pinprick of light at the end of the tunnel.

During that season, the support of our families bringing groceries and spoiling us when we came to visit made things seem less scarce, but the growing pains of learning to live on only what we had were tremendous. We sold both our cars, humbly and gratefully accepting two old work vehicles my dad had available. I began working on job placements with my mom's staffing company and bartered a gym membership for childcare services. We hardly ate out, and we made our coffee at home. Each month, I would gratefully open the statement that showed the red number ever so slowly decreasing.

I will never forget the moment I had to fully accept our reality. Having waited all week for payday, I planned a big grocery trip on my way home from the nanny job I had taken to supplement our income. Ashby and I literally walked up and down every aisle and filled our cart to the brim. We were tired and hungry, but happy to be heading home as we made our way to the checkout line.

As the bagger loaded our mountain of groceries into the cart, the checker turned to me and asked, "Do you have a different form of payment?"

"No, this card should work. Let me try again. Maybe I bumped the wrong numbers for my pin," I responded, shifting my daughter to my other hip. My card was declined.

*No, I don't have another form of payment. Today was payday. There should be money in there.* The thoughts shot rapid-fire through my brain as I scrambled.

"I'll save this transaction. You step right over here and call your bank. We can run it easy once you clear this up," she offered to me kindly.

The banker looked up my account and said that the paycheck was on hold but would be available in 24-48 hours. It was bank policy, so there was nothing they could do. Mortified, I picked up my toddler and walked out of the store empty-handed. I cried the entire way home.

My husband was now an NFL football coach, and yet we still couldn't afford groceries. I knew it was our own fault. We had made so many poor financial decisions in a short amount of time that eventually, we had to start over. Everyone around us seemed to have newer cars, live in nicer houses, go on more vacations, even eat out more. It was humbling to have to navigate a truthful way of looking at our finances, living within our means when it seemed that we *should* have much more than our bank statements read.

It would take a few more years before we would allow this authenticity to permeate the other areas of our life, but the practice of admitting our financial brokenness undoubtedly prepared us for the work to come in our personal life.

# CHAPTER 5

# THE ONE THING

I CHEATED ON LIZZY for the first time at my bachelor party one month before we got married. From the start of our relationship, I was binge drinking and going out with my friends, without Lizzy. Before I was ever unfaithful to her, I was already there in my mind. Bad habits combined with addiction made it hard for me to resist temptation. It was a pattern I knew well before we started dating. Prayer and trying to change my behavior hadn't worked in the past, but I really thought marriage would somehow put an end to this struggle.

Once we were married it wasn't any different. I would be out with my friends and take my ring off, acting like I was single depending on who was around. This didn't happen all the time, but I left a crack in the door for deceit. It was kicked wide open when I got to Seattle. Now I was traveling around the country to play different NFL teams, which gave me an opportunity to go out and explore the nightlife. Even as I write this, I am on a plane heading to Cleveland, Ohio, to play the Browns. The team gives us an envelope with per diem for food, a hotel room to sleep in (alone), and a travel itinerary that is wide open after 9 p.m. For me, this was a recipe for disaster.

Don't hear me wrong: I'm not saying my profession was at fault for my waywardness. However, it definitely gave me more opportunities to make bad decisions. Lizzy would frequently ask me to call her when I got back to the hotel, and I promised that I would. Most of the time, however, I would get back late, so drunk that I wouldn't dare call her for fear of being found out. Instead, I would pull out an excuse: "I didn't want to wake you up." I could tell that this song and dance was getting old, so I started talking to her on the phone until about 10 p.m. Then, I would tell her that I was tired and ready to go to sleep. Once I got off the phone, I would get dressed, call a cab, and go meet up at a bar with friends. After a while, she stopped asking me to call, and I got the sense she knew I was lying to her.

One night in the off-season, Lizzy and I were talking about the strain that coaching can put on marriages. The topic that triggered this conversation was a well-known football coach whose private life had gotten out of control. After having an affair and struggling with alcohol, his wife was divorcing him, and the whole thing quickly became public knowledge. Knowing my own issues, I was not about to "cast the first stone." So, I mustered as much sympathy (well, let's be honest: it was actually empathy) as I could and said, "You never know what issues a person is dealing with. I don't want to judge him simply based on what the media is saying." I felt sad for him, but it also terrified me that this could soon be my reality if I didn't change my ways.

"I can put up with a lot of things, but the one thing I don't think I could ever forgive is if you cheated on me," she replied, sending a dagger straight into my stomach.

I felt sick. It felt like an indirect threat based on all the patterns that were showing up during the travel of football season. Knowing that I couldn't show her how much shame I really felt from that comment, I scrambled to find words to cover up my rising anxiety.

"Growing up in church, I saw lots of people work through these kinds of problems." I was trying to give myself some hope that we would be able to survive if she ever found out about my infidelity. I thought taking an authoritative approach would put her on the defensive and keep her from asking further questions. I could sense that she knew something was going on in my private life and was trying to scare me out of doing anything further.

The truth is, after we had that conversation, my shame brought me to the conclusion that I was never going to come clean. Turns out, the decision to stay silent was the worst mistake I would ever make in our marriage. It was like trying to put out a fire by pouring gasoline on it. It seemed to me that by not bringing it up, I was making the best decision to keep our marriage and family together. I rationalized that if I told her what I was doing, she would leave. How was that going to be *good* for any of us? However, instead of protecting our family, the decision simply separated us further. What I had actually created was a private island where *I* could do whatever *I* wanted to do.

By choosing to keep my private life in the dark, I created the perfect environment for my sin and shame to grow. I heard someone once say, "Shame is the shovel that the devil uses to dig us into an ever-growing pit." This perfectly describes what happened during the next few years of my life. No matter how hard I tried by going to church, reading my Bible, and praying, I always had a secret, dark place that was just mine. Unfortunately, the pit I was digging kept getting deeper, wider, and easier to fall back into.

# CHAPTER 6

# THE OPEN DOOR

THERE IT WAS AGAIN—that same feeling. The one I wanted to push back into the farthest place my mind could wander; the place reserved for ridiculous, middle-of-the-night fears that were clearly illogical as soon as the morning sun hit them. I knew how to manage *those* fears and how to tell myself they weren't true. Besides, there was so much to be happy about: Dave and I had two beautiful kids, a good job, two homes, and a loyal dog. We regularly attended church, and somehow, in the midst of raising a family, I found the time and passion for getting fitter than I had ever been.

Yet, I was still plagued by the feeling that there was something missing—some piece that was the key to this complicated puzzle. Something keeping us from the life we really wanted, and the terrible sensation that it was somehow my fault.

It kept happening no matter how far I tried to push the thoughts away. So, I did what I knew how to do—I worked out harder, focused my energy on our fixer-upper house, had another glass of wine, and took the kids on adventures. I allowed the constant wave of *new* and *more* and *fun* and *better* to keep the tide of fear at bay. On the outside, we were building the life that I always wanted, but on the inside, I was left feeling empty and alone.

The buzz of the phone brought me back to the present. Dave was driving, so I reached down to check it for him. A woman's name I didn't recognize flashed across the screen, so I opened the message and read it aloud to him.

*"How's life in the Pacific Northwest?"*

My shoulders tightened as I braced myself against those familiar feelings.

"Who is this?" I asked as nonchalantly as I could muster, hiding the fear and anger I felt rising in my throat.

"Just a reporter I met at the Combine. She's a friend of another coach from his time in New York."

"Why is she texting you?" My ability to hide the edge in my voice was failing.

"Oh, I don't know. Maybe she just wants to know how the team is doing now that we're back in off-season, and the loss is behind us?" he responded coolly.

"Is she married?" All attempts at covering my distress were now gone, replaced by a smoldering exasperation. I stared out the window, tensely holding to the door handle as if I were bracing myself for what would come next.

"I think so?"

"She doesn't sound married." It was a familiarity in the tone of the text that I had grown to recognize and detest. It was a cutting familiarity that said, "Yeah, I know him. I have access to him, too." I was tired of it. Maybe it was the last few months of finally telling myself the truth, even if only in small doses. Maybe it was the fact that we were stuck in a car for a few hours, and I was too tired to pretend the rest of the way. Whatever the reason, the crack in the door was there, and I took a deep breath and pushed my way in.

"Maybe it's not her, but I feel like you have a door open."

Silence. Suffocating silence. Hot tears spilled down my cheeks as I fought desperately to control the emotions threatening to upend my happy little life. Then, almost at once, that same peace that allowed me to push into the hurt and tell the truth kept the words coming.

"I am tired of this feeling. I am tired of wondering. I don't feel safe in this marriage, and I can't keep feeling that way." The tears continued to fall silently as I willed myself not to disturb the moment and draw more attention to what I had just allowed to leave my lips.

More silence. My body buzzed as the adrenaline surge subsided. We rode that way for a few minutes before he reached over and took my hand. Undisturbed in the backseat with headphones on and a movie rolling, our oldest glanced up with a searching look as I wiped the tears away. The conversation was over, but the words could not be taken back.

——— ✦ ———

Dave: For months, Lizzy and I had been planning a trip to Orlando, Fla., to visit her younger sister Katie once football season was over. I was looking forward to our time together to decompress after a long, exhausting season. But my wife had other plans. After she called me out that night in bed, asking if I was happy in our marriage, I knew that there was a "Where do we go from here?" conversation looming on the horizon like a stormy rain cloud. Right before we left Seattle, she asked me a question that would eventually change *everything*.

"What do you think of going to a marriage conference together after we get back from vacation? You'll have the time off, and it's only three days. Can we commit to going?"

"Of course. That sounds great," I said, already panicking inside. By now, I was an absolute professional at pulling myself together when things were falling apart internally.

To make matters worse, my friend Chris, a pastor at our church, found out that Lizzy and I had signed up for the event. Not thinking anything of it, he asked, "Would you and Lizzy want to be a lead couple at a table to help facilitate the breakout sessions?"

*The last thing we should be doing is trying to help other people with their marriage, but if I decline his invitation, he'll have a feeling that our marriage is "on the rocks." We can't have that happen*, I thought to myself.

We had been to several marriage conferences before. In fact, we averaged about one every other year. We were typically invited to go for free as a way of promoting the event to other high school, college, and professional coaches who could see this as a networking opportunity. At the bottom of the advertisement for the event would be a list of notable coaches.

*Coach Dave Canales (and family), Wide Receivers Coach, Seattle Seahawks.*

I knew this song and dance all too well, but this conference was going to be different. Ever since that conversation in our bedroom, I knew there was no turning back. Something had to change.

I had resolved that I was going to tell Lizzy the truth—the whole truth, and nothing but—about the man she married. And it was hands-down the scariest decision of my life. Even as I'm writing now, I can feel my stomach starting to tighten and the hollow feeling beginning to reappear in my chest and legs. After I decided to tell the truth, it felt as if my feet were no longer on steady ground. How was I supposed to keep this mask on for an entire week?

Well, I did what I always did: *I faked it.* I put on a smile and desperately tried to act as present in conversation as I possibly could so that no one would suspect I had something to hide. I had discovered that if you look interested enough in what other people are saying, doing, or showing you, they are less likely to start prying into your personal affairs. I mean, we all want to be heard, seen, and felt, so I simply offered that in exchange for privacy. Just a little trick I learned growing up in church.

Lizzy's sister and her husband Robbie had been married the previous June and were settled in a cozy little cinder block home in Lake Forest, a suburb of Orlando. We had a free place to stay, Katie and Robbie to act as tour guides, and some extra spending money from our conference championship season. It had all the makings of an intimate time of celebration for both our career success *and* their new marriage. However, a "celebration" is a far cry from where my heart and mind were. On top of the mountain of shame and lies I was hiding, I was going to have to wear the mask for an entire week in Florida. It was incredibly exhausting to live that way, to say the least, and I had been doing that, well... all my life, really. So, what did I do in an attempt to hide my inner turmoil?

I drank. A lot.

On this trip, every meal was an opportunity for me to stay buzzed enough not to feel. It was two or three beers at every meal and sometimes a quick shot at the bar on the way to the bathroom. It was also a lot of fun signature drinks at Katie and Robbie's house. I mean, we were on vacation, after all! Besides, I was much more willing to put up with Lizzy's questions about my drinking habits than I was answering questions like, "What's on your mind? You seem distant. Is there something you need to tell me?"

It turns out, that is what I feared the most: being found out as a fraud.

While on our trip, a good distraction from reality was when I reconnected with a coaching buddy of mine named Luke. Luke and I coached together in Seattle for two years, and Lizzy and his wife Nici had become like family. They had since accepted several promotions, the latest one landing them in Jacksonville coaching for the Jaguars. We arranged a day-and-a-half-long reunion for our young families, which was especially exciting because their son Barrett was born weeks before they left Seattle.

They lived four hours away from where we were staying, but Lizzy and I loved driving together, especially in places that were unfamiliar. We saw road trips as a chance to connect. We talked about the future and did some birdwatching as mile after mile of highway scraped away the calluses of the daily grind we had left at home. With two little kids in the back of our rental car quietly watching a movie, it was the perfect break amidst the nonstop action of our vacation. We popped in and out of conversation, only taking breaks to comment on the landscape or the wildlife. As I drove along during one of these breaks, staring out of the window to catch a glimpse of the native Floridian birds, I received a text message.

*"How's life in the Pacific Northwest?"*

Lizzy glanced at my phone, reached into the console, and read it out loud.

"Who is this?" My gut tightened and my neck tensed, all the blood drained from my face, and I started to panic.

*Who was it?* I thought, trying to conceal the anxiety rising in my chest as I looked at the number.

It turned out to be a female reporter I had met at the NFL Scouting Combine a few weeks before.

"She's a friend of a coach's agent. I met her at the Combine," I said, wondering if she could see the beads of sweat forming around my eyebrows.

"Just a friend? She sounds like she knows you pretty well. Why is she texting you?"

I took the authority-figure approach and said, "In my profession, I'm going to have to talk to lots of female reporters. It comes with the territory."

"I understand that, but I do not see why she is reaching out to you in the off-season. This just doesn't add up."

We went back and forth for a few minutes, getting louder and louder until I finally stopped. I waited a moment and softly said, "I promise you, Lizzy, I'm telling you the truth."

And just like that, the fight was over. With tears silently streaming down her face and a look of utter betrayal that might as well have said "All is lost," she looked directly into my eyes and said, "You may be telling the truth this time, but I also know that you have a door open."

My heart sunk. *You've lost her*, I thought to myself, feeling the mask of my false identity starting to crumble. I was no longer the "Golden Boy" who could do no wrong. All the old tricks I had used in the past to try to win my way back into her good graces were not going to work anymore. The devastating part about this argument was that while my conversations with the reporter had obviously been way too friendly, for once, I *was* telling the truth. That's how I knew she was done.

As I looked out of the window at a loss for words, I panned to the rearview mirror and met the eyes of my little girl staring at me above the iPad. The thought that this could be our last vacation together hit me like a ton of bricks, and reality became all the more present. The moment I looked at my little girl, the anxious feelings I had were gone, replaced by a deep sadness and utter hopelessness that I had never experienced before. I felt my feet firmly on the ground now, but they felt so heavy.

*What had I done?* I imagined moving out of the house and into an apartment. I thought about the statistics of broken marriages and the effect they had on the kids. I thought about the long road back to finding out who I really was underneath the façade. And I was devastated.

That night, instead of pressing into the tension with Lizzy and figuring out what we were going to do next, I went out with my buddy. I left Lizzy at the hotel with the kids and got as drunk as I possibly could in an effort to forget all that had just unfolded.

But I couldn't.

# CHAPTER 7

# DO YOU TRUST ME?

WHEN LIZZY, the kids, and I returned to Seattle after our vacation in Orlando, I went back to work at the football office for the week. With the marriage retreat around the corner, work was a pleasant distraction. Every time I thought about the retreat, I felt like I was staring down the barrel of a shotgun.

I started to have second thoughts about coming clean to Lizzy. In my mind, I still had a chance to do what I always did: act as if the text message from the female reporter was an isolated incident and promise never to let that happen again. I could admit to struggling with pornography or being too casual with another female. That type of issue would hurt for Lizzy to hear, but at least it would force us to connect. Then, we would at least feel like we were doing hard work. As horrible as it sounds, this was the approach I had taken for the entirety of our nine years of marriage—not to mention the two years we dated beforehand.

The problem with this approach—or, rather, one of the many problems—is that, much like visiting the doctor, if you do not reveal *all* your symptoms, it is impossible for them to correctly diagnose the issue. Forgiveness works that way, too. If someone forgives you for *part* of your wrongdoing, are you truly forgiven?

Over the years I was living a secret life, I would somehow always come back to a place of brokenness and repentance before God. I often found myself in this place when I was alone in a hotel room or working out at the stadium before a game, asking Jesus to wash me with His blood. The heavy burden of shame would press down on my chest, consuming my mind about the sinful choices I had made the night before. I would attempt to verbally beat myself up, as if this mess could be fixed by being stronger and more disciplined.

But every time, without fail, Jesus would whisper, "Where are your accusers? I don't accuse you. Your sins are forgiven. Go and sin no more. I have something so much better for you." *That* was the love and acceptance I was so desperately looking for. It was as if I was deliberately trying to ruin my life, and Jesus just would *not* let me do it. The second part was harder to hear.

"Now go and make yourself right with your wife."

There was always some action, some step of faith, that Jesus required me to take to test whether I trusted that His way was better than mine. That is the part that scared me the most. I was hoping that I could confess to the Lord, who is full of grace, and move on without having to involve Lizzy... who may not have been as understanding as God.

From time to time, my dad would preach a sermon out of Matthew 5, focusing on verses 23 and 24. These scriptures say, "So if you are offering your gift at the altar and there remember that your brother has something against you, leave your gift there before the altar and go. First be reconciled to your brother, and then come and offer your gift." (ESV) My dad taught about how, in those days, people sometimes traveled for hundreds of miles, taking up to a week to get to the synagogue. This was a major financial decision for the families involved—imagine all of the money that went into preparing a caravan and traveling with your entire household! Now, imagine having to come up with the unplanned expense of an extra trip home right after you had just arrived at your destination. *That* is how strongly Jesus felt about reconciliation.

The day before the marriage conference, as I was driving home from work along the shore of Lake Washington in our quaint little neighborhood called Kennydale, I was thinking about Matthew 5 again. I remember taking a slight left turn up the hill, driving past the public parking spots that face the lake with the Olympic Mountains serving as a backdrop. As I gradually climbed the hill, leaving the lake behind me and heading for home, it was as if the Lord spoke to me in an audible voice. Again, I heard the words I didn't want to hear.

"Go and make yourself right with your wife."

God knew that I was battling two competing emotions. The primary feeling that I had was the fear of losing my marriage. God knew that I was trying to figure out the right words to say to Lizzy to minimize the damage—which was going to be impossible, given the nature of what I was about to tell her. He also knew that I was excited about all that was going to be unlocked in my life once I was able to reconcile with Lizzy.

"But what if I tell her the truth, and she leaves me? What if I lose my job after I worked so hard to get it?" I fought back. His next reply was a lot less like a whisper; in fact, it much more closely resembled a roar.

"Dave, I don't want your marriage, and I don't want your ministry. I just want you!" The response felt like an arrow piercing straight through my calloused heart. "I'm not promising you that you'll keep your marriage and raise your kids together. I'm not promising you that your career will be successful. But I AM promising you that I will never leave you. I will help you to become the man that I made you to be, and I promise you that no matter what it may look like, it will be better."

As I continued my drive home, I felt the way I imagine Abraham must have felt walking up the mountain to sacrifice his only son, Isaac. You know, the one he had been waiting for all of his life. The one that God had promised him. I was about to risk everything—my career, my family, my livelihood—by being obedient to the call I had blown off for the past 10 years. It was the call to be honest with my wife and ask for forgiveness and reconciliation, and it was terrifying.

There is a cartoon that went viral a few years ago that depicted Jesus lovingly asking a little girl to give Him her tiny teddy bear. The little girl was scared because it was her most prized possession, and she really loved it. The cartoon also showed Jesus with a nearly identical teddy bear behind His back, except it was about 10 times the size. While not seeing the blessing to come from her obedience, the girl heard Jesus say: "Do you trust Me?"

At that moment in the car, I felt Jesus asking me the same thing.

"Dave, do you trust Me?"

However hard it was going to be, I wanted God's blessing on my life, and I was willing to sacrifice my most prized possessions to receive it. I decided that I was finally going to tell Lizzy the truth, risking it all with the hope of what God had in store for me on the other side. Like any person embarking on a high-risk adventure, I was frozen with uncertainty. At the same time, I had never felt so alive.

## CHAPTER 8

# MORE THAN YOU KNOW

ONLY TWO DAYS after the conversation in bed where I finally told Dave I was deeply dissatisfied with our marriage, I joined my weekly moms' group on a Wednesday morning. All was normal until our host invited a guest to make a special announcement. Like a white-hot spotlight shining directly on my chair, I knew with immediate certainty that this was meant specifically for me. I sat trembling in my chair in a cold sweat as I listened to the pastor talk about the marriage conference our church would be hosting. Phrases like "the hardest weekend of my life" and "the best thing we've ever done" reverberated in my mind when he finished. I felt like this was a sign pointing to what seemed the only way forward for us.

Later, when I asked Dave if he wanted to go, I made it clear that I didn't need an answer right away. After all, the last thing I wanted was to drag him there. I still couldn't really believe he had agreed; I was surprised he was willing, a passive admission that we needed help. He didn't even balk at the application process that required answering in-depth questions about our marriage and personal lives. I tried not to think about how he might be answering, choosing to focus on what I was experiencing in our marriage. Being honest with him had galvanized me into being truthful about what I was feeling, so I used the application as a chance to answer for myself only.

It should have come as no shock that we were asked to be table facilitators for the conference—we looked and acted the part from the outside. However, fresh paint and immaculate landscaping couldn't make up for the deeply flawed foundation our marriage was built on, hidden below the surface to those looking from the street. I didn't know we were bracing for a hurricane that was just out of sight, lurking on the horizon. The conference opened on Thursday night, and while the format was similar to other conferences we had been to, this was more intimate and honest from the beginning. The facilitators jumped immediately into an invitation to use this weekend as a time to really talk about our issues and a challenge to not stay on the surface.

Our first activity Friday morning was to spend some time journaling about areas we needed to reconcile with our spouses. Quiet music played as I sat on the carpeted floor searching my heart, hoping to find answers to what was so tragically flawed in our relationship. I was open to any answer and desperate to find what I needed to fix, but mostly I felt bewildered and lost, as if the answer were just out of my reach.

Meanwhile, my husband wrote furiously in his journal a few feet away.

After some time passed, they asked us to partner back up with our spouses. We sat leaning casually against the wall, facing each other, the sunlight streaming down on us from the third-floor window. Feeling guilty that I hadn't found the answer to moving forward, I asked him to go first.

He didn't waste any time getting straight to the point, taking a deep breath as he spoke.

"Babe, I've been unfaithful to you." No beating around the bush, no excuses, just a straightforward statement. He looked me full in the face, the tears welling up in his eyes as he waited for my response.

The world around me faded to gray as I sat waiting for the air to come back into my lungs. My heart shattered into a million pieces in a split second. And, in so many ways, so did our marriage. I finally had concrete evidence that there was a reason for my growing unhappiness in our marriage. Something was tragically broken, and that something was our covenant. Here he was confessing the one thing I had said I would never forgive. Time stood still. I understood *what* he said, but the reality was slow to sink in.

As we sat there quietly, I realized I actually had known, albeit in some deep-down place I wasn't ready to go to until that moment. The tears began to fall silently as I closed my eyes and breathed in the full weight of what he had just revealed. I waited motionless, unsure of what to do or say next. I felt bewildered, like I had woken up in the middle of a faraway forsaken land, completely lost with no idea of what to do next or how to get home.

Much to my surprise, in the stillness, my heart began to change. Like a flower in the middle of a fire-ravaged forest, something new was beginning to grow.

"I know," I breathed, barely above a whisper, my gaze fixed on my hands in my lap. "But I don't want to do this life with anyone else."

The words left my mouth the same moment I realized that my heart truly meant them. This was the man I had vowed to love forever, and, somehow, I knew I had no option to turn back now. Instead of recoiling in pain, I reached for him, and we held each other and cried. The tears unleashed a wave of indescribable emotion, revealing overwhelming feelings of shame, disappointment, and abandonment we had been silently riding for years. This was no quick fix, but more a dismantling of the lie we had been living. We really wouldn't understand the way forward until much later when the dust finally settled from this great implosion.

My decision to stay wasn't an act of heroism to prove that I was strong and could handle anything. It was an act of desperate hope, one that would alter the course of my life. I had no idea how difficult it would be or what it would bring, but this I knew for sure: it was the only path I wanted to take. The following months would prove to be the absolute hardest of my life, but even in the midst of the pain, I could cling to hope that we were going somewhere new. We had started a new trail, down into the valley of the shadow of death that would eventually lead to a brand-new life.

———— ✤ ————

Dave: In preparation for the marriage conference, Lizzy needed to make arrangements for our kids, Ashby and Ben, to be taken care of. While the marriage conference was held at our home church in Bellevue, just seven miles away, Lizzy, in her wisdom, felt it was important to stay at a hotel down the street. I think she could sense that some pretty heavy work needed to be done and wanted to create some space for us to do the lifting. So, we went to our tribe for help. She called her parents to ask them to stay at our house with the kids for two days.

Lizzy is a Seattle native, and her parents, Bob and Margie, lived only 30 minutes away. Her parents graciously accepted our request and showed up at our house on Wednesday evening, the first night of the conference.

We were expected to show up early the first night because we had accepted the role of table leaders. This meant we would facilitate the breakout sessions with the other couples at our table. If you're wondering what on earth I was thinking when I accepted that role…you're not alone. When my buddy Chris asked me if we could facilitate, I said, "Absolutely!" as if I were confident we had a lot to offer. The truth of the matter was, I didn't want to mar the image Chris had of our family and let him down. After all that happened between Lizzy and me in Jacksonville, we should have called Chris to tell him that we were going through some hard stuff in our marriage and could not (*should not*) continue with our role as table leaders as planned. Of course, that would mean admitting that our marriage wasn't perfect, and we weren't about to do that. So, I gave myself a fresh haircut, we packed our bags, and we drove over to the church.

When we arrived, the lights were down low, candles were burning, and worship music was playing. The conference leaders huddled up all of the table leaders and asked the Holy Spirit to move in the lives of all of the couples that were coming. I was in tears immediately, both feeling the weight of my guilt and burdened by what I knew I had to tell Lizzy. I knew that prayer was for me. The leaders walked around our huddle, praying for each couple, and when the woman got around to us, she said, "There is so much grace in her." Then, she leaned in and whispered, "More than you know." At that moment, it was like Jesus Himself grabbed my burden, lifted it off my shoulders, and nailed it to the cross. I felt so safe and free in the palm of God's hands. I knew this was the perfect time and place to lay it all down. As much as I would have liked to just confess everything to Lizzy in that tender moment, I had to move on, trusting that God would provide the right opportunity for me.

That night, we watched some videos, asked questions, prayed, talked, and got acclimated to the rhythm of the sessions. The conference leaders were intentional not to take us too deep into the wounds of marriages yet, just tilling the soil for what was to come. As the night came to a close, we were given homework to do when we each got back to the hotel, so Lizzy and I explained the exercise to our table, and we all left for the night.

The hotel we were staying at just so happened to be the Seahawks team hotel we used on the night before our home games, which felt intentional—this was the first of many things the Lord wanted to redeem for us. While I tried to be engaged in conversation with Lizzy that night, there was one line on the agenda for the next day I had my eye on. It was a breakout session on reconciliation. Though I didn't know what it was going to look like, I knew it was the time to tell Lizzy the truth.

The next morning, the leaders opened up the floor for couples to share what they had talked about in their hotel rooms the previous night. There were a lot of tears and some incredible breakthroughs shared. We then watched a few video testimonials of couples talking about their experience during the reconciliation session, and my heart started racing. I knew it was time. Our leaders informed us that we would have an hour to break out as couples, and we were given the option of walking around the church campus or finding a quiet corner in the chapel. We opted to stay inside and chose a space next to a window looking out on a beautiful spring Seattle day.

We sat down on the floor, and when I looked into Lizzy's eyes, I started to cry. With as much of my voice as I could muster up through the tears, I eked out, "I've been unfaithful to you, Babe. I'm not the man you think I am."

With tears pouring down her own face, she said, "I know. I've known for a long time."

I knew what she meant by those words. Though she didn't have physical proof, I knew that she knew intuitively that my heart and mind were somewhere else. Then she took my hand and said, "But I don't want to do this life with anyone else." I had never experienced the love of Jesus so tangibly in my whole life. In a split second, I understood what the Apostle Paul meant in Romans 5:8 when he wrote, "While we were still sinners, Christ died for us." What an incredible picture of grace and unconditional love. If Lizzy, as a human, could show me that kind of grace, I could only imagine how much more Jesus poured out (and continues to). I sobbed in her arms as time seemed to still, and heaven and earth collided full speed.

I felt immensely free and, for the first time in my life, truly known. In the coming years, a friend asked me an intriguing question: "Are you open to the fact that you may have become a Christian that day?"

I have to say that it certainly felt like that was the case. I was saved at a "Power Team" event when I was 11 years old, but that day, at age 33, I felt truly sanctified. It was the most tangible experience of grace I ever had.

The healing process of infidelity—or any lies within a relationship, for that matter—is a very complicated one, that's for sure. What we would learn a few years later in counseling is that my healing began the day that I confessed to Lizzy.

However, though I had grieved all of those past experiences in the moments they happened, for Lizzy, who was just learning about all of my secrets, it could take years to work through all of them. Lizzy would now have to go back to the beginning and reframe every memory of our relationship for the past 10 years. Her grief would come in devastating waves as she realized the layers of deception that I had built up in our marriage.

The fact of the matter is that neither of us really understood how long the road would be. During the two years after the marriage conference, I felt as if I were sitting in the car with my bags packed, keys in the ignition, ready to head out on a new trip... while Lizzy was just starting to unpack her bags from our last one.

———— ❖ ————

Lizzy: You might be wondering what it felt like the moment Dave told me we'd been living a lie. I had never caught him red-handed, but when he finally came clean, I felt two things: relief and shame. Looking back, I realized the signs were all there, yet I also realized how good I was at ignoring them. Mind you, he didn't go out often, and he covered his tracks well, but when he did go out, it felt like he could turn off the "partner switch" in his brain and totally disregard me. It was the little things like going to the next bar with our friends and sending me home alone when I was ready to call it a night, or continuously not checking in on the road when I knew he was going out.

How could I spend nine years wanting to believe we had a good relationship only to have his devastating secret life come tumbling out of the shadows in a mere minute? Even more terrifying to me was that somewhere, deep down, I always knew, but I had never really wanted to find out the truth. How could I have so little self-respect that I was more comfortable ignoring this behavior instead of confronting him, despite how much I hated it?

The truth is, his behavior just inwardly confirmed what I already believed. While Dave wrestled with the decision to expose his secret shame, I wrestled with another giant: the fear that, deep down, the reason he was out galivanting like a single man was because, ultimately, I was a disappointment. I believed that if I were better-looking, sexier, or more adventurous, if I did more and brought more to our marriage, then he wouldn't want to be out drinking with the boys. Yes, his decisions were despicable. No marriage should ever have to overcome the devastation infidelity brings. But I would have struggled with some of these feelings even if he had never stepped out—fear that I could be replaced, that I would ultimately end up alone.

With each experience in which I was left to fend for myself, insignificance ate away at my sense of security. Like stones being added to a backpack, it was becoming heavier and heavier with the weight of living this mostly happy but tragically flawed journey. I rationalized his behavior and looked for the positive, trying desperately to keep my head above water. I lived from one vacation to the next date night, clinging to the Instagram reel of highs that made this shaky, heavy load seem worth it.

So, why didn't I come to some sort of ultimatum or dig deeper into what was really going on? Well, more than I feared uncovering his suspicious actions, I was afraid I would find out I really wasn't worth changing for. I was terrified that what he was seeking when he was out, doing whatever I was not invited to be a part of, was more valuable than protecting me and my heart. Deep down, I think I truly believed he thought he had made a tragic mistake by choosing me. If I were enough, he wouldn't have a desire to be anywhere but home with us. And day by day, these "ifs" were slowly and secretly eating me alive.

From the get-go, I knew our marriage wasn't going to be perfect, but I was convinced we had enough to figure it out together. I figured if I could just work hard enough, sacrifice enough, love enough, and *be* enough, it could see us through. However, nothing could ever be "enough" to overcome his addictions. Only one thing is strong enough to free people from the bondage of sin, and that is **the blood of Jesus, His work on the cross**. My love was never going to be enough to free him from his slavery, but God's love could. I was looking for my husband to save me from my own prison of loneliness and insignificance when what we both needed was to be set free from our wounds, lies, and brokenness.

This brokenness kept us locked in a vicious cycle of disconnection. The first few years, the dream of a career in football kept our eyes forward, shoulder to shoulder, chasing after success. We hoped together, played together, worked together, talked about almost everything together, but never turned *toward* each other to do the deep inner work of reconciliation. Then we added kids, moved up the career ladder, and were busy creating a dream to share. The more responsibility we had, the easier it was to ignore our shallow relationship. We wanted to be out in the deep, but we were stuck running around in ankle-deep water. We were missing the most valuable gift marriage has to offer: being fully known in the middle of our ugliness and, somehow, still being unconditionally loved.

I didn't know how to be vulnerable with my fears, so I ignored anything that pointed to my inadequacy in the hope I wouldn't be found out. Like a child who thinks shutting their eyes will make the scary monster go away, we ignored the symptoms of our deteriorating marriage while every chance we had at true intimacy disappeared into the hidden world of secret shame. In a moment, the bondage of this terrible agreement was broken, the truth cutting through it like a double-edged sword. It would take years to recover, the consequences of our choices woven throughout the fabric of our marriage.

But the power of darkness was broken.

# CHAPTER 9

# NOTHING HIDDEN

IT STARTED THE VERY FIRST NIGHT Dave and I got home from the marriage retreat: reclaiming enemy territory. Earlier that morning, we basked in the warmth of a glorious Pacific Northwest spring morning, looking out at the glass-top lake. The scent of wisteria floating around us mingled with the peace we felt from knowing we were no longer hiding from each other. The hollow echo of the truck door slamming brought me back to the icy reality of what we were facing, and the earlier peace I felt began to unravel like the edges of the blankets covering the seats of his vintage Chevy. The sunshine of the spring day was quickly fading, and I felt a new chill creeping in through my fractured reality.

We arrived home to our 4-year-old daughter in hiding, the result of an unexplainable meltdown with my mom. Dave crawled under the bed with her while she ranted and raved. I waited outside the door and heard him gently praying for her as her yells turned to sobs, eventually slowing to sniffles. Soon after, they quietly joined us to eat dinner on the porch, Daddy with his daughter perched peacefully in his arms. We gave my parents a vague explanation of how great the weekend had been, thanked them for babysitting, and settled the kids into bed for the night.

The darkness of what we were now facing descended on me as I climbed into bed that night. I sat staring at the closet, nauseated by the realization that my husband's wardrobe—clothes that I had purchased for him—had taken part in the violation of our sacred covenant with each other. I suddenly had an overwhelming desire to start a bonfire right there in our room. Images began to flood my mind of darkness and deceit, and the unraveling continued. I was frozen in dread, as if a heavy blanket had been placed over my shoulders. It had been one thing to talk about the brokenness in our marriage at the conference, tucked away from the rest of our life, but now I realized I really wasn't equipped to handle everything I had learned.

My husband could sense me sinking into the pillows, the oppressive weight of darkness paralyzing my thoughts. Neither of us had any idea what to do now, alone in our room without any outside help. How did we begin the process of repairing what was so tragically torn? He began to pray quietly. I sat numbly beside him, overcome with the desire to run as far from that house as I possibly could but unable to move a muscle. After a few minutes, he paused. Turning toward me, he said, "This is going to sound strange, but I have a picture in my mind right now of Jesus trying on my clothes."

I was shocked, snapped back into the moment by his words. I hadn't said a word to him about the thoughts racing through my mind, and yet here he was speaking directly to them. I unclenched my fists and jaw, willing my stomach to settle, and relaxed my shoulders. Tears spilled onto my cheeks as I released the pain of returning home. We weren't fighting against the things hanging in our closet or the bottles of alcohol in our pantry. This was a far more sinister enemy strengthened by the choices we had made and the lies we believed about our true identities. Even though our life drastically changed in a single weekend, most of the daily details of life remained the same. Dave went back to work the Monday morning after our marriage conference, and life clicked on. After dropping the kids off at school, I came home to a house full of dishes, piles of laundry, and a garden full of weeds. The house felt stifling, and I needed fresh air, so I headed outside. I noticed that an area of newly turned-over ground where we were hoping to grow grass had been taken over by weeds, and I knew it was the perfect project. Gloves on and ponytail swinging, I set to the mindless task of ripping out the invaders.

I was beginning to see some real progress when a text came through from Dave. "Hey, Babe. I just put a chew in, and I know I have lied about that in the past, but I wanted to tell you because I didn't want to keep it a secret from you. I'm not ready to quit yet, but I wanted you to be a part of it."

Instead of feeling compassion, I looked down at the weeds crawling across the dirt, and I felt my jaw tighten. I reached down and pulled the first tendrils of seemingly innocuous morning glory from the fresh brown dirt, only to find that it was the only visible part of the vine. The root snaked its way halfway across the lawn, finally coming completely out on the other side of the yard. Each time I grabbed a small handful of the weeds, I ended up with an armful of roots, and the pile steadily grew larger. The smallest ones had the longest underground trail, and those that were beginning to blossom were the hardest to pull out.

As sweat beaded on my brow, I became more and more infuriated with the hostile takeover of unwanted growth. I wasn't going to leave anything in that dirt, and I knew why. I wasn't attacking the weeds. I was attacking the lies and habits that had threatened to ruin our relationship. I literally began speaking out loud, in my garden, a mantra with each section I annihilated.

"Nothing left to grow. No place hidden. Everything turned over," I breathed aloud as I obsessively raked my hands through the soil. I was committed to whatever it took to get these weeds out.

When I spoke to Dave that afternoon, I didn't hold back. "You've been set free. No longer a slave to fear. You don't have to keep anything of that old life. You don't need tobacco. There isn't any room for any of that anymore." I was angry that we had been duped for so long, buying into the lie that half-truths or omissions weren't that harmful. The lies were invasive, the intensity and freshness of the entanglement fueling my bold attack on anything hidden. I wasn't condemning him; I wanted to speak truth and life. To my relief and gratitude, he responded by throwing away the tobacco and he expressed the willingness for any other stronghold to be exposed.

The days and weeks following that first victory were more like tactical, hand-to-hand combat as we sought out the traps of the old ways and found our way forward into the new life. Slowly, our home was becoming our safe haven—the place where we could control what came in and out. Out there in the real world, we were bombarded by the remnants of the old decisions, hidden mercenaries seeking to entrap us in the past. We knew the past wasn't going to go quietly, and we were fighting for our life together.

More reminders of the old ways popped up out of the freshly overturned soil and we were ruthless about yanking them out before they had any room to take root. On a hike one afternoon, Dave received a seemingly innocent text from a female acquaintance we both knew. His phone was in my backpack, so when I handed it to him, I saw her name on the marquee across the front screen. He deleted it on instinct. That same anger flickered inside me, igniting questions about their involvement and why he deleted the text without saying anything that swirled in my mind. Instead of seething by myself, I caught up with him a little further up the trail and asked him about it. He took my hand as we kept walking, his warm hand anchoring us to each other. He invited me into his inner turmoil, describing *his* reaction when he saw the text. His disgust with the old way of casual familiarity with other women and the shame of his past made him want to hide reflexively, fleeing as quickly as possible from the sickening feeling of being caught.

These conversations led to a decision that no matter what either of us was feeling, no matter what he had hidden before, it was best to just talk about it when something else that we had buried came up. This was not an easy process for me. Each admission, each uncovered lie was a fresh wound. Just when I was starting to feel like one was beginning to heal, I was scraped raw again. But I knew we had to expose these raiders of intimacy. As painful as it was to expose long-hidden lies, covering them again would have interfered with the healing process, allowing secrets to fester and eventually maybe even grow into habits again.

Each season in football brings familiar patterns, events that reoccur annually, which now gave us a chance to reclaim enemy territory. We weren't cavalier. There was no bar table ministry, late nights at the club talking to people about Jesus or beers with the guys. These places are straight-up landmines for my husband, and we couldn't afford any more casualties. Instead, we decided to be intentional by reclaiming the unavoidable hangouts that had become pitfalls because of addiction and division. We started reframing those times into what God had intended them for all along.

Road trip weekends became virtual dates for us. While I would have loved to travel more with him, we have four young children. But thanks to technology, what was once a chance to check out and go about our own agendas was now an opportunity to experience intentional connection. I put a movie on for the kids, and Dave and I spent time on the phone going over the week and whatever else we missed in the midst of the crazy hours of his job. I still feel the fear rise up at times—the sadness at what we lost during the other years—when he goes on the road. Now, I have the fullness of what we experience on this side as balance.

We've been intentional to reclaim memories that were tainted by the past. Family vacations had renewed meaning. Birthday parties gathered our tribe without the overwhelming entanglement of alcohol. We reframed relationships with former accomplices to shame. We even had children together again. We find incredible joy in remaking memories in places (and with people) that once held secrets and pain.

The lingering sting of infidelity remains. In many ways, I hope we always remember the pain of being prisoners of the war for true identity. It makes waking up without a hangover all the sweeter, and the battle worth fighting every time some adversary comes seeking to distract us from where we are headed. Sometimes I wish healing was a one-and-done process, but I know now that a life of ease is not truly what I want. We are, all of us, caught up in this epic fight for justice, and it is a gift to see that clearly now.

# CHAPTER 10

# WHAT ELSE?

THE CONFERENCE HAPPENED to fall on the very last weekend before the off-season normally picks up speed. Reality hit like a freight train that very next morning as Dave headed back to the office, and we found ourselves trying to balance the demands of the spring football schedule while bearing the weight of the painful truth of our broken marriage. Other than the few people we opened up to at the conference, nobody close to us knew what was going on. I did not know how to ask people into my pain. Involving anyone else was terrifying, and I vacillated between wanting to protect my husband from what people would think if they knew and wanting to run away and hide myself. I questioned everything in my life. Nothing seemed to be true or certain anymore, like the rest of my world could evaporate into a mist at any point. I was fragile and consumed with surviving the trauma of my broken heart, but I had to march on. I had two young kids who couldn't understand what was going on, and I wanted life to feel the same for them. Most days, it ached just to breathe. It was even more painful to smile and carry on polite conversation when everything inside me felt shattered. I wore my armor of pretending it was all OK until the kids were in bed and I could let the whole charade go for a few sweet hours. I was bone-weary and depressed.

I had never experienced anxiety before, but suddenly the last place I wanted to be was in public, especially if there were other women around me. I remember wondering if every beautiful woman I encountered was someone he had secretly had an affair with. Anytime we were out, even something as simple as running an errand together, I was afraid he would be recognized. I was on high alert constantly. We went to a Mariners game together one sunny evening, and the minute we walked through the stadium gates, all I wanted was to go home. The laughter around me felt like a jeering insult, my pain distorting this happy family event. All I could see around me was a seething mass of destruction in the form of beer, flirting, and people grasping for relevance. To his credit, Dave was nothing but gentle with me whenever I was overtaken with fear. He never made me feel guilty, just took my hand and tried to be there with me.

In his initial disclosure, I learned enough to know that when we weren't together, whether at home or on the road, he had been open to the possibility of someone else. He was willing to answer whatever I asked, but instinctively, I knew I couldn't handle much more detail than a vague picture of his other life. Life moved forward, but I was lost in the jungles of broken trust, not knowing which way to go.

This shrouded understanding lasted for two months until late one night, right before the start of vacation. I was up alone, packing for our annual summer kickoff road trip to the Ketchum Kalf Rodeo. In the silence of my sleeping house, the chaos in my mind slowed. Dave was going to be home for the next month, and we would finally have space to process beyond the nightly tearful conversations as we collapsed into bed exhausted. Suddenly, I wanted to know *specific* details about the events and memories that I had long forgotten but never made sense to me. I made the initial decision to reconcile at the conference, but now I needed to know what it was I was actually forgiving. Going forward, I didn't want any secrets, and I could no longer live without a clear understanding of his life, our life, for all of those years.

As we loaded everyone into the car the next morning, I knew this drive would be different. The thing I most looked forward to about our trip every year was the way it took us away from the busyness of the city. It felt like we were able to take a deep breath for the first time, climbing up through the majesty of the Cascade Mountains before descending into the quiet rolling hills of Eastern Washington. An hour into the five-hour drive, winding through the canyon carved by the Yakima River, I felt the urgency to ask the questions that would piece together whom I had been married to for the past nine years.

"Did your cheating only happen while you were away, or was it here, too?" the first question tumbled out of my mouth, sucking the air out of the car. Gripping the steering wheel, he slowly, truthfully, and painfully answered.

"Do I know any of them?" The questions came one after another, his answers severing every hope I was still holding onto that some intimate part of our marriage had been a sacred place. The heaviness descended upon the car, and our sadness grew. Tears streamed down both our faces as my husband confessed and relived the life that he had kept hidden. As the 45-minute drive along the river merged back onto the main highway, I exhausted my list of specific questions and asked, "What else?" It was as if he had been given a key to unlock the dungeon of his deepest secrets, the doors flung wide open to expose the shame locked away in his heart for many years. Eventually, his words gave way to quiet worship music playing softly on the radio. We rode in silence, and I wept until I had no more tears to cry.

Despite the devastation of that conversation, there was a new freedom emerging between us, and it was beautifully lifegiving. Peace mingled with the pain as I realized that, for the first time, I really *knew* my husband. No longer was I in love with an idea of the man I hoped he was—an image he allowed me to believe was true. Now, I was free to love the man underneath the mask, brokenness and all. Not once did he try to excuse himself; he just spoke the unabashed truth, and it was like a breath of fresh air. The further we got from home, the further we traveled from the old life we knew of leaving things unspoken. By the time we arrived in Glenwood, we were utterly spent, emotionally and physically. However, I felt at peace that I now knew enough. Not that there wouldn't be more questions, but I finally had what I needed to move from the agony of grief to the next (and equally as challenging) step: forgiveness.

———— ✦ ————

Dave: After Lizzy and I attended the marriage conference, I had no choice but to hit the ground running. Mid-April for the Canales family means spring football, and I was back to long hours at the office. It means two months of intense training and meetings, preparing for the upcoming summer camp and fall season. To add additional stress to the situation, I was promoted to wide receivers coach—a promotion that I had been working toward for years, but one that meant a lot more responsibility. Lizzy and I spent every night for the next six months talking, crying, and praying. However, we didn't have any big blocks of time to process all that had happened.

As spring football was coming to a close, we started to look ahead to the summer months, which were always kicked off with our annual Father's Day weekend family trip to the Ketchum Kalf Rodeo in Glenwood, Wash. Lizzy's Aunt Molly started the tradition a few years before, and we always looked forward to it. The rodeo was the perfect break from the non-stop action of work and school. Fresh mountain air, wild cow milking, and Indian fry bread tacos—what more could you ask for? The week leading up to Father's Day was also the last week of school for Ashby. This year was a bigger deal for her because she had a "Moving Up" ceremony, going from preschool to kindergarten. It was a cool, perfect, sunny day in Seattle, in the mid-70s. It might shock you to hear a Southern California boy like me call a 70-degree day "perfect." Let's just say my standards have changed since living here; all we are looking for here in Seattle is no rain. After a short ceremony for Ashby, we loaded up into our 1999 Suburban (affection-ately known as the "Millennium Falcon") and hit the road. With a 5-hour drive ahead of us, my joy and excitement for Ashby quickly turned into a sobering anticipation of the heavy conversations that lay ahead for Lizzy and me. Different than our last long drive in Jacksonville, I was not nervous or afraid because I had nothing to hide. As we left "the city" in the rearview mirror and headed into the mountains, I was ready to go deeper with Lizzy.

Driving on I-90 East through the densely treed Snoqualmie Pass, trading skyscrapers for evergreens, felt like the pine nee-dles were scrubbing away, mile after mile, all the muck accu-mulated from living the "city life." The further we drove east, the more I could feel my hands on the steering wheel loosen up, my shoulders relax, and my mind start to expand beyond the Franklin-Covey planner on my desk in the office. By the time we reached the Yakima River Canyon, the highlight of the drive, I felt relaxed enough to take in all its splendor. There is a certain reverence about the canyon I feel every time we drive through. The speed limit of the highway slows down to a crawl at about 45 mph, forcing you to take it all in. Regardless of the weather, you *have to* roll the windows down. You can both hear and feel the silence, interrupted only by the sound of the rushing water. From bald eagles to osprey and an occasional deer, and even mountain goats scampering on the high golden hills on both sides, it truly is a sanctuary.

By a sure act of providence, there couldn't have been a better place for Lizzy and me than right there in that temple. We were about to have a conversation that would change everything. You see, a few days after the marriage conference, I told Lizzy that I was willing to answer any questions she had about my secret life. I also asked her to pray about the level and depth of detail that she wanted to know. While I knew that the truth needed to come out, I also knew intuitively that excessive details about what had actually transpired could cause unnecessary (and lasting) damage.

Lizzy was ready to go deeper, and I was ready to press into her. Up to this point, she had not asked me many of the details of my unfaithfulness, but it felt like it was time to talk about it. Enough time had passed from the initial shock of finding out that I was cheating on her, and I was ready to answer any questions that she had.

She mentioned that, at different times over the years, when I would come back from road trips, she could sense I was hiding something, and it was as if the Holy Spirit was directly guiding her as she navigated through her memory bank. She nailed every event. I told her what happened and with whom. Some of the women I was involved with were close to home and some far away. I told her the darkest and ugliest secrets of my life—some so dark I don't want a single other person to know. The winding road rocked us tenderly, worship music playing through the speakers as we cried and talked all the way to Glenwood.

The last thing we needed to address before we saw Lizzy's family was how and when to tell both of our parents.

"The rodeo is *not* the best place to tell my parents. I want to avoid becoming the center of the weekend," Lizzy said. There was a lot to celebrate in the family: babies being born, marriages, job promotions, and retirement. Lizzy was being thoughtful about not putting a damper on all that was happening.

"I want to be the one to tell people. I feel like it's important for me to own up to my decisions." She gave me her support. This moment was so important because it was another chance for me to carry my own burdens. I could sense that as I made more decisions like this, I would continually build up emotional currency with Lizzy.

"The first ones I want to tell are your parents. Since I asked them for your hand in marriage, I should be the one to ask them for forgiveness in breaking my vows to you," I continued, sure it was the right decision. We agreed that we would tell them when we got back to Seattle.

As we pulled up to the long, half-mile, gravelly drive to the cabin in Glenwood, I parked the car. As is our tradition, I let Ashby sit on my lap so that she could drive up to the house. We usually honk the horn obnoxiously, announcing our arrival, while Ashby or Benjamin clumsily try to keep the Falcon on the road. In the midst of the commotion, a flood of mixed emotions overwhelmed me. At first, I felt a lot of shame, having the nerve to show up here again to one of her family's most sacred weekends. At the same time, I felt lucky that Lizzy was willing to give me another chance to do this the right way.

Even though we decided not to talk to the family about all that had happened between us over the last six months, I still felt nervous, wondering if my mother-in-law would use her intuition to figure out that something was very wrong. In spite of all of the negative emotions, there were two thoughts that comforted me. The first one was that *Jesus loves me, and He'll never leave me.* And the second one was that *Lizzy loves me and is committed to working things out.* Whenever those fears welled up in my head again, those two thoughts made me feel hopeful that this marriage was going to work.

In retrospect, what was so special about that weekend was that our story belonged to just the two of us for a little while longer. If you are going through a hard time in your marriage, maybe even struggling through the aftermath of unfaithfulness like Lizzy and I were, I want you to know that your story belongs to the two of you and no one else. It may seem hard to believe, but Lizzy and I are strengthened by the memories of the hardships we have been able to overcome with God's help. In fact, some of our best memories have come from weekends like the one you just read about.

There's a photograph from that weekend in Glenwood I love because it's the perfect metaphor for our marriage—both then and now. It's a picture of Lizzy and me right outside the cabin in our workout gear, running in full stride with huge smiles on our faces as we look up at kites 10 feet over our heads. What the picture doesn't show is that it was a windless, hot afternoon, and our kids were crying because the kites we brought from Seattle would not fly. But Lizzy and I, instead of just saying, "Too bad, I guess it's not kite weather," decided to do something about it. We sprinted around the house to keep the kites in flight, in hysterics, for about an hour. While I am sure everyone in and out of the house was entertained, that's not why we did it. Lizzy and I were making a statement to each other that even though we may not always have kite weather, we will be committed to finding a way to make them fly. With our marriage in God's hands, we knew that anything was possible.

# CHAPTER 11

# UNCHARTED TERRITORY

WITH THE SUMMER MONTHS COMING, there was another difficult conversation on the horizon. Lizzy and I had a trip to L.A. to see my family coming in three weeks, and we would be staying at my parents' house. It was important to me to tell my parents about all the change in my marriage, and to be honest, I was *terrified* of having this conversation. It was important to tell them because we wanted to form authentic relationships from here on out. We wanted to start with being truthful with each other, then to our kids, then our families, and then let that way of doing relationships overflow to anyone we met.

My plan was to tell my parents everything. Not any unnecessarily graphic details, just the truth about my unfaithfulness and that Lizzy and I were walking through a really tough time in our marriage. While I was terrified of telling my parents, feeling like a little boy who was in trouble, the conversation

Lizzy and I had on the way to the rodeo gave me the courage to commit to it. After telling Lizzy my deepest, darkest secrets, I felt brave enough to talk to anyone about anything. This was a major growth moment in my life. I had always talked a lot, but now, I was speaking from my *heart*.

Though it was new territory for me, to be truly known was an indescribable feeling. Lizzy's Aunt Molly once told me, "The truth is when your head, heart, and mouth are all saying the same thing." After the drive to the rodeo, I finally began to understand what she was describing.

As we got closer to traveling to L.A., I had a lot of resentment building up toward my parents. I was going through an all-too-common season of soul searching, and it led me to question my upbringing and whether my parents had really done all they could to prepare me for life. This is a common part of maturity which, I have to admit, was happening for me a lot later in life at the age of 33. I was finally learning how to accept total responsibility for the pain that I had caused. To be honest, I was looking for someone to blame other than myself, and at the time, my parents were the target.

As soon as my parents picked us up at LAX, Lizzy and I asked to take them to lunch. We chose a Mexican restaurant at the Redondo Beach pier and settled into the table. I was getting nervous, waiting for the right space to start an incredibly difficult conversation. We made small talk, eating chips and salsa and tableside guacamole. Once we got our food, things started to quiet down. The kids were busy coloring, and I saw my window.

As I started telling them about the marriage conference, my eyes welled up with tears. Immediately, I felt like I was 5 years old again, confessing to them about something bad I had done. I was not sure what kind of reaction to expect but I was hoping for sympathy. To my dismay, both of my parents looked shocked, embarrassment quickly spreading across their faces. While I was hoping for compassion, I saw from their body language that they were carrying a sense of failure as parents. Almost as quickly, their faces turned to sadness and confusion, which made me realize that I had completely misjudged how they were going to respond. Words cannot adequately describe the depth of abandonment I felt at that very moment. I was inviting them into my heart, and it felt like they didn't want to go there.

Underneath the feeling of being completely unseen, I started to get angry. I was sad because of my own hurt, but I was furious that my parents had not even acknowledged what my wife was going through.

It was precisely at that moment that I realized what was happening. I had let my parents believe in a false image of who I was. They saw me as a Christian influencer, a young coach on the rise with a perfect little family, and I had just shattered that picture. I took off the mask, and it was difficult to handle. I felt completely misunderstood, as if the real me wasn't good enough, and it was something I was getting accustomed to as people began to find out who I really was underneath the façade that I had put up for most of my adult life.

Like many people, I grew up in a home where it wasn't safe to talk about hard things until something snapped, and it was clear now that had played a huge role in how I dealt with conflict. My parents' reaction reminded me that as a family, we were good at talking about our accomplishments but not about our failures. There was a lot of pressure growing up, feeling like I was competing to be in the right all the time. That type of home environment does not produce people who can easily be vulnerable with each other. Now, I had recreated that model in my own family, and my relationship with Lizzy was suffering the most from it.

"Are you guys OK now?" my dad asked, breaking the silence.

"No," I replied. "But we are going to stay together."

My parents and I have since talked about that day, and I apologized for my immaturity and lack of empathy. After writing this section, I realized how selfish it was of me to just dump all of that on them in that kind of setting. If I could do it all over again, I would have met with just the two of them at home, not at a crowded restaurant. We needed so much more time and space, physically *and* emotionally, to properly process something as traumatic as infidelity and serious marital issues. I would have also gone in with the understanding that I cannot control how someone reacts to the things I share. And I would have tried harder to put myself in their shoes.

Lizzy: We waited until we visited Southern California that summer to share our struggles with Dave's family, knowing this was information better received in person. When his parents picked us up from the airport, he asked to go to lunch before heading back to the house. Up until this point, we had given no indication that there was anything going on, so our conversation was going to come at them out of left field. We both felt it was best to tell them immediately and give them space and time to react without any other family around.

We were all tucked into a booth, one child on either side of me resting on my lap after our flight. The table was just tall enough that I couldn't lean into it. I sunk awkwardly into the cushion, feeling small and apprehensive, thankful for the sweet sleeping forms of my 2- and 4-year-olds snuggled warmly beside me. I was pretty sure it would be almost as devastating to them as it had been to me.

Dave didn't waste any time. Over a bowl of chips and tableside guacamole, the story began to unravel. He spoke candidly, starting with the conference and his confession to me. As we listened to him retell the events of the last few months, a wave of heaviness washed over the table. Yet again, everything that we had successfully hidden gave way to the truth of our broken relationship. His words were like a brick, shattering the image his parents had previously held of their son. Their reaction was a mixture of sadness, disappointment, and confusion.

I remember pieces of the conversation, but mostly I recall feeling far away, as if I were watching this scene unfold from afar. As Dave finished recounting the last few tumultuous months, we all sat motionless and silent, no doubt trying to be present but each dealing with our own inner distress.

"Are you guys OK?" his dad asked cautiously after a few moments, snapping us all back to the present. As Dave began to talk about the work we were doing to repair our relationship, I ached in desperate, consuming grief. This wasn't a conversation to wrap up neatly. Nobody could say anything to make it go away or find the silver lining to end on a good note. It was just raw and ugly and hard. Like unwanted guests who arrived when no one was looking, shame and loneliness crowded silently into the booth with us.

No one really knew what to do or say next. We pushed our food around our plates, appetites and conversation lost in the awkward silence, the only noise emanating from the buzz of restaurant activity in the background. After a few minutes, I made myself busy making sure the kids had eaten enough and took them to the bathroom. We awkwardly gathered our things, someone paid the bill, and we emerged from the dark, quiet restaurant into the dazzling Californian summer sun. We walked slowly along the pier to the car, the beautiful weather a stark contrast to the storm of emotions we just weathered at the table.

This was the first of many truthfully hard conversations with our families. Looking back, I can see that was a conversation Dave and his parents should have had alone. It was unfair to ask them to respond to this life-altering information on the spot. At the time, we were desperate and broken, stumbling through this confusing fog, trying to find our way into a new life. Nobody is really ever prepared for this kind of lost. In our longing to be united, we assumed that we should just have all these conversations together. Finding out your son has been living a double life is hard enough, much less having to do it in the presence of your daughter-in-law and grandchildren.

Not to mention the fact that *I* was in the middle of grieving the pain of my *own* shattered heart.

I now know we complicated the healing process by asking other people into it, and yet we didn't know what else to do. We were simply riding the waves of overwhelming emotion, each day bringing a new challenge with harrowing, heart-and-soul-threatening decisions to be made. We were bound to make mistakes as we navigated a storm we were totally unprepared for. This wouldn't be the last time we wished we would have handled conversations differently. Thankfully, we were surrounded by people who were willing to be gracious to us as we stumbled through, their love and forgiveness helping usher us into a new place where brokenness gave way to growth. The lessons learned in our darkest hours became shining beacons of hope for the good to come.

# CHAPTER 12

# HORNET'S NEST

LIZZY AND I LOVE TO GO HIKING. For us, living in the Pacific Northwest is like being kids in a candy store; you can hike a different trail every week! One of our favorite hikes is Chirico Trail in Issaquah, Wash. It is a short but treacherous hike about two miles to the top, lined with old-growth evergreens and ferns. The smell of the fresh damp earth and the trees, especially on a misty day, is infinitely better than diffusing eucalyptus and pine oil. Having grown up in L.A., I fully believe the fresh air is slowly reversing the damage done to my lungs from all the pollution!

On this particular summer day, Lizzy and I loaded up the Millennium Falcon with Ashby, Ben, and our dog, Kuma, to hike up the trail in the late morning to beat the heat. The hike was challenging, as usual—we had just finished climbing "steps," which is a stretch of the trail where forest rangers used native rocks to dig in 2-foot-high steps, which is basically like doing 200 box step-ups in a gym. We were breathing hard and loving every minute of it. After winding around a few bends, we were stopped by a 30-something-year-old couple.

"Just a heads up, in about 500 feet, there is a massive hornet's nest off to your right. It blends right into the branch it is hanging from, so be careful," the man said.

"Are the hornets active?" I asked.

"No, but I'd have the kids stay on the trail and not throw anything in that direction."

Lizzy and I thanked them for their kind warning and proceeded slowly past the nest, keeping Ashby and Ben on the far side of the trail. As we continued at our kids' pace up the trail, I explained to them how considerate it was of that couple to warn us of a potentially deadly situation, given that I am allergic to stings. We all walked in silence for a while, and suddenly, a thought popped into my mind. It was like a vision of the future for Lizzy and me that I could see clearly in my mind's eye.

I saw Lizzy and me walking along a trail together with our hiking packs on, and we were looking for people to talk to. We had scars all over our arms and legs from a bad run-in with a hornet's nest and were stopping married (and unmarried) couples to warn them about the danger ahead. I kept walking over to the men, saying, "See that scar right there? You are heading to the same place where I got that one. You do not have to go down this path; there is a better way." While I was warning the men, Lizzy talked to the women and showed them *her* arms and legs.

The thought of sharing our scars with people was so energizing that it seemed like a calling that we were headed toward. In real time, the vision that I had on the trail happened in the span of about two to three minutes, but it seemed like much longer. I think it was the significance of the moment that made it seem like time stopped moving. These types of moments, I have come to learn, are like traveling to another dimension—you think you were there for years but return home to find it's only been a few minutes. Like going into the magical wardrobe in *The Chronicles of Narnia* or Platform 9 ¾ in the *Harry Potter* books. As we continued hiking, I turned to Lizzy, excited and out of breath, and said, "That's us!"

"What do you mean?" she asked, not understanding what had just transpired.

"Lizzy, we are going to be just like that couple. We will stop people who are heading toward the same danger that we just came out of—we'll show them our scars!" I shared the rest of the vision with her as we neared the top. As she looked at me, I could sense the fear and excitement in her eyes. While there is eternal purpose in sharing our scars with others, it would take great courage to tell our story. We had to really think about how exposed we would be as a couple who already existed in a very public profession. Sharing our scars meant being willing to tell people the truth of how our marriage failed. The challenge for Lizzy, which I did not fully understand at the time, was that she felt like a fool for not seeing what I was doing behind her back. She felt stupid as she looked back, knowing that there were women in our social circles I was involved with sexually while she walked around as if we had this great life. If we made our story public, what else would come to light that would make her feel even more like a fool? She confessed to me recently that she was even afraid someone was going to show up someday with a child saying, "Dave, this is ours."

I had no idea how scary this proposition was to Lizzy. I was too caught up in my excitement to help couples just like us—couples who needed to know that there was hope. My enthusiasm for sharing our story also came from wanting to make sure that my mistakes were not made in vain. I knew that there were millions of men out there who were stuck, hiding because of the wrongs they've committed and the lies they've told. I wanted them to know that I didn't wake up one day and decide to cheat on my wife. It happened over time, starting with little white lies hidden in the dark that grew like a fungus. I wanted to be able to say, "I've been down that trail, and I got stung pretty badly. You don't have to go that way." I wanted them to know that there was another way—the way of truth. I wanted them to know that although the trail is steeper and more challenging, it will all be worth it when they get to the top. Most of all, I wanted them to know that they are not alone.

# CHAPTER 13

# FULLY KNOWN

IN THE EARLY MONTHS after my husband disclosed his secret life, he felt an incredible sense of freedom from being finally being known. I, on the other hand, was terrified of people knowing what was really going on.

Even though we allowed a few people in to see the full reality of what we were walking through, I was still struggling with major anxiety concerning what people would think of me for choosing to stay with Dave after his disclosure. I imagined all the things that might be going through their heads:

*Of course she is going to stay. How is she going to get anyone else that amazing to choose her?*

*He loves her because she didn't leave him. He made a mistake, but he can't leave her now—not after she decided to stay.*

These thoughts were irrational, yet they were mentally and emotionally debilitating.

Clearly, his choice to step out was not my fault, but I felt certain that it wouldn't have happened if something wasn't really wrong with me. He had obviously looked to other people for excitement, beauty, adventure, and pleasure. *If I were enough*, I thought, *he would not have made those decisions*. My deepest fear had been confirmed: I was not worth fighting for. For so long, I had assuaged those fears by going along with the happy image we were projecting. While our relationship was fun and some parts of it were even really satisfying, I had been living with this hidden dread throughout our entire marriage.

On top of the mounting anxiety, I felt isolated. I was afraid to talk to my mom on the phone for very long for fear she would ask too many questions, and it would all come tumbling out. I was hurting deeply, yet I couldn't let the people closest to me see it because of what I feared it would open up for them. In my fragile state, I wasn't equipped or prepared to handle the fallout. To make matters worse, most of the people I interacted with on a daily basis had no idea about this inner turmoil. The few people who *did* know were incredibly empathetic, but they couldn't carry my pain. Without experiencing the ravages of betrayal, there is no way someone could understand what I was going through, much less have any idea how to help. With so many raw emotions, I constantly felt as if I were on the verge of a breakdown.

I didn't realize it at the time, but I didn't want to tell people because I knew I couldn't manage their responses. My life was in shambles. As a person who avoided personal pain to a fault, I didn't want to feel my people respond with *their* pain as well. It was hard enough to be in constant contact with my own, and I needed as much normal as I could find. I went to CrossFit, took the kids to school, made meals, walked our dog, and worked on house projects. I held my babies, counting down the hours until Dave got home. When he was there, I could finally be real with how I was feeling. I wasn't afraid of his reaction, and I didn't have to filter my emotions or wonder what he was thinking. We could just sit in it together, raw and messy though it might have been.

The one voice that felt true and safe enough to trust in the middle of this time was Jesus, through the words of the Bible. God felt closer and more real than ever before. Worship music gave words to my pain, and I played it all day long. Every time I turned on Pandora, without fail, it was as if the unspoken cry of my heart was coming through the speakers, my wounds laid bare through the music of the artist's utter desolation. I spent a lot of money on iTunes that season, carefully crafting the playlist of both my hurt and hope. As I let the Word and worship wash over me, a little seed of hope started to grow. I didn't know how, but I was beginning to truly believe that one day, I was going to heal and be whole.

I couldn't explain why, but I was desperately afraid to tell my family. Of course, I was afraid that they would be angry with Dave. But what I feared the most was what I was supposed to do when they turned all their attention to me. All my life, I had been the one to bring wisdom in situations riddled with pain and confusion. Self-confidence, however false it had been, was my calling card. My sense of humor buoyed people when they were feeling helpless, and I could find a silver lining in just about every situation imaginable. I learned early on that my skill of rolling with whatever punches life threw at me was valuable to people; however, that also made me feel like it wasn't safe to be messy or undone. Now that I was the one underwater, I had no idea how to call for help. I had built my identity on having it together, and now I was a spiderweb of cracks, ready to shatter at any moment.

After the rodeo weekend, we decided it was time to invite my parents into our journey. Dave was off for the summer, so this was our best chance at having space and margin to process with them. We asked them if we could come up to their condo to have dinner, that we had something we wanted to talk to them about. They knew our time at the marriage conference had been powerful, but we hadn't told them much more than that. Though they had been around us enough to see that things were different, they hadn't pressed or asked for more than our vague descriptions of how good the weekend had been and how we were doing in the months that followed.

After the meal, we settled the kids into a movie and moved outside onto their deck with a sweeping view of Puget Sound and Whidbey Island. The setting sun cast glorious golden light around us, and the moment felt sacred. I braced myself as Dave opened himself up and began telling my parents our story. I sat quietly as the truth unfolded, perched high in the barstool chair. I let out the breath that I had inadvertently been holding, my fingers tracing circles around the rim of my wine glass. They listened intently as he disclosed the man that their daughter had really been married to all these years—the one underneath the mask.

When he finished, there was a pause, and I cautioned a glance up. I was surprised not to see any malice or anger on my parents' faces. I was even more shocked when my mom reached across the table and took Dave's hands. Looking him squarely in the face, she said with tears in her eyes, "I'm so excited for you! This is the best day of your life! Now Jesus can really do His healing in you." His shoulders softened, the grace and relief of her response cutting through any lingering fear and shame.

My mom's experience of grace as a young woman—when her life seemed to be over because of the choices she made—colored her response. She knew just what it felt like to be at the brink of everything collapsing and having grace and mercy open to a life full of more joy than she ever dreamed possible on the other side. Now that he had bared his soul, she was finally free to be honest with him. Dave had kept her at arm's length for as long as she had known him. Knowing her past, he was afraid she would be able to see through the mask, and it made him uncomfortable, to say the least.

"There is nothing more freeing than being fully known," she responded. Without blinking an eye, she continued. "Also, I never trusted you fully. I've told Lizzy that, and now I know why." She wasn't being mean, just honest. I could see from his response that Dave felt that it was a fair statement.

Amid the tears, apologies, and joy, my dad's response was gentle. "All of us have struggles. Your sin is no worse than anyone else's. We still love you. Nothing has changed because of this new information." He responded to Dave as a dad to a son, not a father to a wounded daughter. He was concerned for me but did not try to step in and protect me. They have always made it clear that this was our marriage and that we had to figure out what works for us. Even in this, my dad respected the boundaries of a married couple and didn't try to rescue his little girl. The healing at the table was immediate, and their acceptance was a gift to both of us. I realized I didn't have to prove I was making the right choice.

Over the next few weeks, we planned to tell each of our immediate family members in person. My sisters, brothers, aunt, and uncle responded authentically from a place of deep love for both of us: love, anger, and hurt all mingling together with the new revelation. People rallied around us in ways we could never have imagined, and for the first time, I could sincerely feel how important my people were on this journey. Despite how broken we were, we somehow knew there was incredible value in inviting people into our mess. It scared me to death when it came time to do it, but I knew it was the right plan. Our purpose for telling them wasn't to have anyone fix it. We just didn't want to tell people in 10 years what we had survived. We wanted to invite them into our journey to heal and grow *with us*. We were deeply longing for the relationships that would be forged through the fire of what lay ahead. Now,

I can confidently say that this terrifying process has produced some of our richest, most gratifying relationships.

———— ✦ ————

Dave: While we were at the rodeo, Lizzy and I decided that I would talk to her parents when we got back. We knew we wanted to meet Bob and Margie (Lizzy's parents) up at their place in Mukilteo, Wash. On the way home from the rodeo, I called them and invited ourselves over and told them, "I have something I want to talk to you about." Margie would say to me later that I left her in great suspense, waiting to find out what was so important to talk about. You see, the last time I asked to speak with them without saying what it was about was the time I asked for Lizzy's hand in marriage!

The Mukilteo house was a special place for us. It was our getaway when family life was crazy. We drove up there on a beautiful summer afternoon. From their main floor, you could see miles and miles of the Puget Sound and the south end of Whidbey Island. It was a comforting reminder from God that there was an abundance of grace here. I was beginning to understand what King David said in 2 Samuel 22:20. It was after God had given him a great victory over the Philistines when David said, "He brought me out into a broad place; He rescued me, because He delighted in me." (ESV)

Imagine being in the heat of battle, where you are constantly on high alert. People are dying all around you, and danger seems imminent. Then, imagine you are suddenly transported to an open prairie on a warm afternoon, much like the scene from *Gladiator* where Maximus is running his fingers through golden waves of wheat in perfect peace. That's a pretty radical change of scenery, right?

The Mukilteo house had always represented a "safe harbor" for our little family, whether it was through financial crises or work-related issues. It was a place I always felt at peace. That being said, I was definitely nervous, but at this point I had 10 years of relationship with her parents to lean on. I knew their scars and how long it had taken each of them to get to where they were at that moment. I was going to "cash in" on our 10 years together in a few minutes, hoping that they could find it in their hearts to forgive me and walk alongside us as we began the journey of healing and restoration. So, Jesus, being the romantic that He is, set the backdrop just perfectly. Bob and Margie were sitting on the back deck, enjoying the sun setting over the Olympic Mountains with a glass of wine. The kids were downstairs playing, and suddenly, I was in that "broad place" again.

I joined them outside, by myself, and took a deep breath. Without much small talk, I cut to the chase.

"I've been unfaithful to Lizzy."

As I explained more about what that meant and how the marriage conference had been the catalyst for this conversation, their faces remained surprisingly calm. I told them that Lizzy and I wanted to stay together and work it out, and we were on the same page moving forward. As I shared this, tears began to well up in the corners of their eyes. I did not take Bob for the kind of guy who was going to throw me off the balcony or anything like that, but I half expected him to calmly ask me to leave! Margie was the one I expected to have a more vocal, if not aggressive, response to what I was saying, but when she did respond, I was shocked.

"I am so happy for you, Dave! That's all I can say. I am so happy," Margie said joyfully, tears welling up in her eyes.

Wait, what? I just told my wife's parents that I had cheated on her, and they were happy for me?! I was expecting anger, hurt, and disgust, but instead, I got empathy. Bob spoke next, and it was equally as surprising.

"We all have our stuff. I'm just so happy that you want to stay," he said calmly and lovingly. "In fact, I was afraid you were thinking about leaving Lizzy." Their responses made me feel incredibly loved and seen. I knew then that they loved me for who I was, not just because I loved their daughter. Wow.

Here were two people who have lived a lot of life, walked through some truly trying times as individuals, and made it through with God's help. It was as if they were passing on the grace that was shown to them. On the drive home, I heard that echo again in a whisper: "I just want you."

How fitting that we spent our last night up at the Mukilteo house while I have been writing this chapter. Bob and Margie (now Pops and Gigi) are moving on to new adventures, and they asked for our help packing up the house. On the last night before they had to move out, we all sat out on the back deck one last time. We crammed our now family of six on that deck, along with Lizzy's pregnant sister, Katie, her husband Robbie, and their 3-year-old, Harper. We thanked God for that place, remembering all of the good and bad times. As I started to say my piece, I choked up. With my voice quivering, I thanked them for being a safe harbor. A place where we could get out of the storm and tie up our wreck of a ship without judgment. I am forever grateful.

# CHAPTER 14

# WHAT BRINGS YOU IN TODAY?

THAT NIGHT AT THE RESTAURANT in L.A. with my parents, Lizzy and I had circled the wagons around our little family as we tried to do something new. The old way of doing marriage and parenting I had grown up with in my big, beautiful Mexican family had failed us in my mind, and I was ready to change everything.

The surest way Lizzy and I thought we could change things was by making everything very black and white in our commitment to seeking the truth. A better way to say that is we became legalistic, meaning that if anything in our life was remotely immoral, we erred on the side of taking it out completely. A good example of this is how strict Lizzy and I became in monitoring the type of music we listened to or the movies we watched. We couldn't tolerate anything crass or sexual in nature, as it brought up too much pain for the sexual promiscuity that I had been involved in. I know that we offended my family in many ways by what we blatantly avoided participating in. I am sure it felt, to them, as if we were judging them. Looking back, I feel sad about the way we did this. I know that we put a lot of strain on our relationship with my family in our attempt to do things differently. We were operating out of a spirit of fear and insecurity, which stemmed from going into uncharted territory as a married couple.

As we returned to Seattle, more "hard" was waiting for us. The healing process for Lizzy was still in its early stages, and the more we talked, the more layers were being peeled back. Our conversations were like a river steadily eroding the bank away, exposing the roots and rocks beneath it. The next layer was exposed when Lizzy asked me a question that had an easy answer, but one that was incredibly hard to say out loud.

"I have something hard to ask you. Was any of your sexual activity unprotected?"

My heart dropped. "Yes," I said, taking a breath. "Lizzy, I am so sorry."

I could see Lizzy struggling to hold back tears as she remained focused on the point of asking the question. There was not much more to say. I was still buried underneath a ton of shame about the decisions I had made, and I got a sense from her that she could feel the weight of it. She didn't ask me any of the details about what had happened, and as her face relaxed, she said, "After talking with my tía Etol, I think we should set up an STD test with our doctors to make sure we are both OK."

I agreed, of course. Not that I had a choice, but I knew that this was a tremendously wise, practical decision. I immediately called my doctor and set up an appointment. In retrospect, it wasn't super painful for me to go to a clinic filled with people I didn't know. In fact, my doctor wasn't even going to be there! But, for Lizzy, it was a different story. She was going to see her regular gynecologist, whom she had known for years.

On the way over to the medical office, Lizzy stared out of the window and said, "I want to tell my doctor exactly why I am coming up to have a full STD panel done." In hindsight, there are two things that I now realize were happening here that make my wife so amazing. The first thing is that Lizzy was asking for my consent to tell her doctor the whole truth about what happened. She did not have to, but she included me in the process, which made me feel loved and respected. This has become a regular practice of ours—to check with each other before we involve anyone else. The second thing about my wife here is that smack dab in the middle of her fear and shame, she wanted to share our story with her doctor. She was thinking beyond the patient/doctor relationship; Lizzy wanted to connect with her as a *person*. While most of us could only think about ourselves in a situation like this, she was thinking about the long-term relationship she had with her doctor and wanted her to know the full story.

Before we arrived at the clinic, a phone call came through. It was my dad. I answered the phone and found that it was both of my parents calling to see how we were doing. After some light conversation about the kids and football, my dad asked casually, "What are you guys doing?"

"We're on our way to see Lizzy's gynecologist to get a full STD panel done," I said, matter-of-factly. My mom launched right in.

"That's smart. You know…" she started, clinically explaining the risks and percentages involved with STDs. Fortunately (and at times, *unfortunately*), my mom is an expert in all things medical. She had been a nurse for over 40 years, which means that she has seen *everything*. I remember coming home as a teenager to all her presentation posters on childbirth, venereal diseases (that one still haunts my memory), and the like lying around the kitchen table. My sexual education happened through osmosis, and the downside was that talking about sex was merely clinical to her. Most of the time, I felt like a patient instead of a son. This was not all bad for me as I was, and still am, very interested in the medical field and sort of geek out on all our bodily functions.

My dad's response to hearing about our appointment was rather victorious. "Praise God!" he boomed, celebrating us for doing the right thing. This made me feel angry and unseen, but instead of reacting that way, I somberly said, "Dad, this isn't a happy or victorious thing for us. This is embarrassing and humiliating. We are sad right now."

To his credit, he understood the pain that caused me right away and apologized, saying, "I'm sorry, Mijo."

Then, something amazing happened. It was as if a long, rainy Seattle week had been interrupted by five minutes of sunshine. He opened up about his life and marriage struggles with my mom. Don't get me wrong; my parents told my two brothers and me about their childhood, how they met, and their early financial struggles in marriage… but they never told us about their *personal* struggles.

There was something different in my dad's tone that I had never heard before. He was talking to me not as his baby boy, but as a man who shared the same struggles. We had something real to talk about beyond our kids and our jobs. It was as if the sun was shining fully in my face, but I didn't want to blink or look away for fear of losing it to the clouds again.

As I got off the phone, my joy quickly turned to sadness, and I turned to Lizzy.

"Why didn't he ever tell me any of this before?"

I felt alone again, and I was downright angry. I was mad at the fact that my dad chose to allow me to believe that he had never struggled. It felt like he chose his comfort over my growth. I figured since he never talked about his struggles, that I shouldn't either. It made me feel like I was just supposed to talk to God about them and move on, never fully sharing what was going on.

It makes me think of a recent hike I was on with my buddy Brett. When we reached the vista point, we were both hit with a metaphor for our relationships with our dads. Normally, on a beautiful day, you can see the snowcapped peak of Mt. Rainier, the mighty Olympic Mountains, and all of Lake Washington at once—*and* the skyline of downtown Seattle settling in the foreground. On this misty, rainy day,

Brett and I saw a wall of white clouds. I mean, we were literally in the clouds, and we had about 10 feet of visibility. The vista point felt like standing at the edge of a cliff with no idea what was beyond it. As we were standing there staring into the abyss, with a look of deep understanding, Brett said, "My relationship with my dad feels a lot like this. Like he's brought me as far as he can, but he's not willing to or doesn't have the tools to go any further."

"I know exactly what you mean," I said, no further words necessary.

As I sat there in the car after hanging up with my parents, I thought about what I really wanted. I didn't want a dad anymore; in fact, I hadn't needed one for a long time. I wanted a friend who was uniquely qualified to give me perspective on the things that might come up next as my life unfolded. What was my dad thinking about when he was 33 years old with all the irons he had in the fire? He was trying to keep the church afloat, working his tail off to finish his Ph.D., and raising three little boys. What about his marriage? My mom worked like crazy, helped direct the church, gave my brothers and me everything we needed, and all of this while my dad was battling underlying health issues. As I tried to put myself in his shoes, I realized what a challenge this time of his life must have been. My resentment started to melt away in light of the newfound empathy I felt. Then, a hopeful thought hit me, and I realized I had unearthed a deep longing welling up from the depths of my soul.

"What if we can do this next part together?"

That's what I really wanted.

It hasn't been an easy process with my dad. I've learned that it isn't fair to expect someone to walk the same path as you or at the same pace. That type of expectation will only make them feel judged and alienated. It's unrealistic to think that any of us can walk stride for stride with another person, but, at the same time, it shouldn't keep us from trying. Now, I have to warn you, though: It is extremely exposing and vulnerable to ask someone to walk alongside you in a truthful, authentic way because you'll run the risk of being rejected or, even worse, betrayed. But it is the most rewarding part of an authentic relationship to be able to truly celebrate someone's growth when you've shared your respective struggles along the way. That is the type of love that Jesus models for us. I hear Him saying, "I will meet you where you are, and I will never leave you."

Over the years, I've realized that loving like Jesus is what matters most. Accepting people for who they are, where they are, and meeting them there consistently, always willing and ready to go deeper. That has been my approach, not just with my dad, but with any other relationship. I have committed to meeting people where they are, and I will always ask these two questions:

"What's next for you?"

"Is there anything you need from me?"

That conversation with my dad helped me crystallize some thoughts about my relationship with our children. I turned to Lizzy and said, "I want to share our story with our kids in doses in an age-appropriate way." Lizzy agreed that it would serve as an opportunity to make us more human to our kids—imperfect and in need of grace. We did not want our kids to grow up with an incomplete understanding of who we are. We hope that by the time they become sexually aware, they will know our whole story.

And with that, she agreed, got out of the car alone, and walked into the clinic. Then we waited for the results.

———— ✦ ————

Lizzy: The call from Dave's aunt came after we returned from our trip to Los Angeles to tell the family. Knowing full well the long-term health effects of promiscuity from her career as a midwife, she wanted to make sure she talked to us as both a loving aunt and a medical professional.

"You guys know that I love you very much, and I am proud of you for the decisions you have made to stay together. But you need to go see a doctor and get checked for STDs. And don't go to a clinic; please go see your doctor. They need to know what you have been exposed to."

It was a punch to the gut. Her courage to challenge us to know this part of the long-term consequence was a gift, but also incredibly heavy. I knew she was right, but deep down, I was also afraid. What if they found something? What if we wound up with more to deal with than the already exhausting emotional consequences? We made appointments for both

Dave and I with the realization that this was the next step in moving forward, but our new freedom felt tainted and over-shadowed by the possibility of even more devastation.

Dave and the kids waited in the car while I went in to see the doctor. Sitting in the exam room felt stark and impersonal, and the drafty chill through my hospital gown went much deeper than my skin. This was the same office that I waited to hear my now 3-year-old son's beating heart for the first time, a place of joy and comfort, a place I planned to come to have more babies. Now, I was waiting to hear if I even *had* a future that included more children.

The nurse practitioner bustled in happily.

"So, what brings you in today?" she asked, scanning my charts.

"I'm here for STD testing." I felt hollow and small.

"OK…" She paused. "What is your level of exposure?" Her question begged for more of the story. I took a deep breath. She needed to know so she could be thorough, but I still wasn't prepared to share my pain yet again.

"Well, my husband recently confessed to cheating on me off and on for the last nine years, so I guess pretty much everything?" The tension that followed seemed to immediately suck all the air out of the room as she looked at me sadly.

"What is it with these men?" she seethed under her calm exterior. I understood her disgust. Up until the last three months, my reaction would have been similar. Until it became my reality, I didn't have to see someone who cheated as anything more than a selfish, insensitive jerk either.

I took a deep breath and squared my shoulders as best I could. "I want to tell you that we have decided to stay together. I don't want you to feel badly for saying that. I get it. I feel that way sometimes, too. But I really know that we're supposed to be together, as painful as this is. And he is asking for help. That is part of why I am here today."

She looked me straight in the eye and gently said, "Well, I think that is very brave. I don't know if I would be able to make the same decision. You are an amazing woman."

The rest of the visit was as routine as possible. Instead of judgment, the nurse had seen me and entered into my world for our brief interaction. She gave me the instructions that the test results would take up to a week and not to worry if I didn't hear something right away. I knew that my anxiety would not dissipate until I knew either way. She was polite and kind, and we both lingered, not knowing how to end the interaction in a way that gave gravity to what had taken place in that room. Giving my hand a gentle squeeze as she left the room, she offered her hope that we would indeed find our way to something better. I dressed quickly and headed back to my waiting family, still feeling sad but thankful to have the appointment over with. The rest of the week was to be spent grieving the need for these appointments, anxiously awaiting the results.

Before we knew what this week would hold, we had scheduled new family photographs for the end of this incredibly sensitive week. This was Dave's idea, wanting documentation of these days, photos to look back on one day when our kids were grown and we could see what God had in store for us. I was a tangled mess of emotion. On the one hand, I was thankful that my family was still intact. On the other hand, there was so much uncertainty about the future, including our physical wellbeing.

We chose St. Edwards Park as our backdrop. It is both majestic and rustic, a little slice of tangled wilderness in the midst of suburbia. Originally a logging site turned Catholic seminary and retreat, it was finally converted into a state park. As we explored one of the many well-worn paths through the woods, we stumbled upon the perfect place: an old prayer grotto more than 100 years old made of large river stones carved into the hillside. Our photographer, who would eventually become an intimate ally and friend in our journey, perfectly captured our family. My favorite picture is of Dave holding the kids on his lap, looking together at the Bible he held cradled between them. It will forever remind me of the weight of that day: uncertain of so much, but desperately hoping for a chance to heal and move forward into something better.

As we packed in the car to leave, we got a phone call from the doctor's office while we were still in the parking lot. Holding our breath, we listened to the results: negative for HIV. The nurse continued down the list of everything else we had been tested for, each with another negative result. The floodgates of relief broke as tears flowed freely down my cheeks; a fully clean panel was more than I had been hoping for. I felt an overwhelming sense of gratitude for the unseen protection I received when I was unaware that I even needed it.

With this report, we had a renewed sense of possibility. The spark of hope was now a small flame and the beginnings of the fire that would burn away the old life and make space for something altogether new. We began to make plans for the future again, daring to believe we were, in fact, going to make it. A short time later, we got more surprising news.

I found out I was pregnant.

# CHAPTER 15

# APRIL 15

TO BE PERFECTLY HONEST, I spent most of that first year merely trying to survive the constant bombardment of heartbreak while somehow finding a way to maintain a "normal" life for my kids. It was harder when Dave was gone at work, mostly when I was going through my regular daily routine. I'd be doing the dishes or folding laundry when all of a sudden, a wave of grief would come crashing in over me. While driving down the road headed for a school pickup or a quick trip to the grocery store, faces and dark memories would take over my thoughts. I tried to stay as busy as possible because the quieter the world got, the louder the truth of what my life now was mocked me.

The greatest sadness for me was all that had been lost, namely joy and security, in everything we shared the first 10 years we were together. He had a hidden life for as long as we had been together, fighting his own darkness far before we ever met. Now that I knew what his life had really been like, every memory we had together felt tainted. I would be thinking back on a birthday or a trip, driving through a part of town we loved, or recalling a conversation when I would realize that even in those times, he had been lying to me. The color would slowly drain from the memory, and I would be left feeling lifeless and fractured. In those moments, nothing felt like it had ever been or would ever be true again.

One cold January morning, I was home picking up the kitchen after the whirlwind of making breakfast, packing lunches, and getting the kids out the door for school. I had music playing quietly in the background when my ears perked up to the lyrics swirling softly around me. Rushing to make it to the chiropractor before preschool pickup, I quickly downloaded the song without listening to it fully, grabbing my journal and purse as I headed out the door. With my headphones in, I put the song on repeat as I wordlessly checked in for my adjustment. The sagging office chair in my treatment room became a sanctuary as the words pierced through the protective layers of my pain. I scribbled the lyrics into my journal while I waited, knowing something was happening that I couldn't quite explain.

"Let this be, where I die. My heart with Thee, crucified. Be lifted high, as my kingdoms fall. Once and for all. Once and for all." Her powerful voice sent waves of understanding through all the hurt and confusion. I held back my tears, not ready to share the sacred transformation that was happening in my heart. As I drove the familiar route to school on autopilot,

I sensed the holiness of this moment. I knew I had a decision to make. This was the crossroads of everything I had dreamed my life would be and what it really was. God wanted to use this to do something miraculous, but I had to choose to let go of what I wanted it to look like. No more fairy tales.

"Let this be, where I die." All that had happened, all that was revealed, all the pain, all the lies, all the shame, all the brokenness of our story was where the crucifixion mattered.

"My heart with Thee, crucified." If I didn't surrender to the death of my marriage, if I kept looking for a way to make this all not true, it would never have a chance to come back to life. This idol had to be smashed to pieces. This was the place where I had to share in the suffering of losing it all in order to be a part of the beauty of rebirth.

"Be lifted high, as my kingdoms fall. Once and for all. Once and for all." I felt my heart break as the reality of dying to my plans, my experiences, my dreams, my comfort, and my expectations became undeniable. I turned the car onto the same exit I had taken every day for the last two years on the way to preschool, and yet, that day, it was all new to me. I had passed through some invisible but very real barrier, ushering me into a place of surrender.

In the quiet of this place, I understood what the Lord was telling me. "This will always be your story. It is no longer your future, but it will always be where you came from. You can't run from that. You can't run from this pain. But you can let Me make that into something beautiful. You can trust Me to see what I can turn this into, in *My* way."

I had asked Jesus into my heart as a tender 3-year-old on the way to preschool many years before, but this was different. This was the moment I truly gave my life to Christ. This was the moment I exchanged pursuing my happiness and comfort above all for the chance to be a part of something bigger than me. It was the moment that changed my trajectory and brought my heart back to life.

—————— ✦ ——————

Dave: After what felt like an eternity, Lizzy and I finally got our STD test results back. By God's grace, everything came back negative. It was a great relief to both of us, but it still seemed like such a small victory in light of the real healing that needed to take place in our souls. With football season just days away, everything got put on hold. We weren't going to have time to sit together and process life with the hourly and daily demands of the season. And, honestly, I was looking forward to a mental and emotional break from all the heaviness in our home at the time.

Coaching football, just like many other jobs, has a way of consuming your time and energy; it can completely take over your life if you let it. For some, it is a great place to hide from the reality waiting for you at home. Instead of an escape, what came next was about two years of long, sleepless nights. Both of us alternated staring up at the ceiling from our bed, wondering how on earth to move forward when all we had was six hours a night.

The way I remember most of that season is it was mostly Lizzy who couldn't sleep. You see, while I was the one living the secret life all those years, she had to relive every memory with new eyes. I knew that my role was to fill in the blanks as they became evident to her. She cried almost every night. And when she wasn't crying, she was depressed. She would talk to me about the things she saw every day that triggered her emotions. For example, Lizzy could drive by a certain part of town where she knew I used to go drinking, and it would cause her to painfully imagine me sitting in one of the bars hitting on other women. All I could do was be there with her in that bed. There was nothing I could say that would fix it, so I simply rolled over toward her, put my hand on her back, and tried my best to comfort her.

Those sleepless nights felt as if we were looking at a 10-year-long photo album, altering the background of every picture. The new information Lizzy had about me forced her to change all our memories. However, the memories didn't change much for me because I was secretly tormented behind the manufactured smiles. I suppose the pain I had caused Lizzy was finally starting to affect me the way it was supposed to. Not only was I incredibly sad for Lizzy, but I was sad for the scared, lost little boy in the photos. But, as my empathy grew for Lizzy, it also started to grow for myself.

———— ❖ ————

Lizzy: When I found out I was pregnant with my third child, Bea, it seemed like every buried fear began to bubble up to the surface. Was I making the right decision? Shouldn't I make him prove to me that he was worth trusting first? Did I really want to have a relationship built on conditions? How would I ever know if I could trust him? What was the balance of faith between God's protection and being downright stupid? What were people going to think? All of the questions swirled together in a fog of unknown. There was no way to truly know what the future would hold, yet I did not want to live afraid and miss the opportunity for the family we both wanted if everything did indeed work out.

Dave began the process of reconciling with my family that summer. He told my big brother Todd, who was gracious to my husband but also made it clear that he was angry about the decisions Dave had made. Dave was thankful for his willingness to forgive him, yet he also understood my brother admitting that, in the moment, his first response was wanting to punch him in the face. I mean, I didn't blame him.

My brother reached out to me to meet for lunch at his office a few weeks later. Todd is a fairly reserved person, so I was thankful he was honest with Dave and intrigued by his offer for lunch. As we sat eating at the conference table on the 17th floor of his office building downtown, I was surprised at how direct he was.

"I think it is really cool that you guys are trying to work through this, and you are willing to forgive him," he paused before continuing matter-of-factly. "Just please do me a favor and don't have any more kids while you are figuring all this out."

I swallowed my tacos dryly. I knew I had a decision to make. Should I tell Todd the truth and risk his disapproval and judgment, or should I stay at surface level and not invite him into my current turmoil? I didn't want to make him feel uncomfortable, but surface-level relationship, especially with people I really love, wasn't an option anymore. All of this flashed through my mind in an instant as I sat pondering my next move.

I couldn't figure out how to say it with any more tact, so I let the words tumble out of my mouth before I could stop myself. "Well, here's the thing. I'm seven weeks pregnant already."

Without skipping a beat, my brother's body language shifted. He smiled, relaxed his shoulders, and sat back in his chair. "Well, OK, then. This is good. I'm happy for you, and I'm totally behind you and Dave having this baby."

His response was sincere, and I could sense his genuine willingness to let go of his idea of how we should handle the future and shift to what was at hand. While his anger at my husband and loyalty to my protection made me feel seen and loved, his immediate switch to love and support was equally powerful. Watching people respond to Dave's deception made it clear just how deeply we were all affected by the lies. My sisters both cried, the elder also confessing that she couldn't imagine our family without him while simultaneously promising to kill him if he did any more damage to me.

The reality that I knew—that my family and friends experienced from us—was unraveling with each retelling of the story. As we invited people into our new life, the consequences of the hidden hurt we both carried reached much further than our personal experience. No one in our circle was left unaffected. It was as if a bomb went off in our family, uncovering different hidden hurt each of us carried, our transparency triggering the same process in the ones willing to engage in *our* process.

Even though everyone had different opinions and reactions, the chance to experience having a child together again, this time without the guilt and shame of his secrets, gave me joy. In spite of the fear, the tendrils of hope were beginning to spread from the start of the new marriage we were growing. I had spent nine years facing only the parts of my marriage that felt good or didn't scare me too much. In choosing to stay, I couldn't ignore our brokenness, but it also meant moving forward with life, leaving the old behind without conditions and punishment. As we shared the news and my belly grew, people responded across the spectrum, from tears of joy to deep concern.

April came quickly. I began to dread celebrating our anniversary. I wanted to celebrate that day at the conference as our new beginning instead. Our willingness and ability to turn toward each other and examine what wasn't working had grown exponentially in the last year. It was still too painful to spend much time thinking about our first nine years of marriage. I felt foolish when I recalled my life before, to think of how I had poured myself into what I wanted to believe was a good marriage. All those memories felt tainted now, and I didn't know how I could honor a day of hollow vows—*and* pretend that it made me feel happy.

Early on the morning of April 15, I woke up to the first wave of a contraction. My due date wasn't for another three weeks, so I wasn't sure that these contractions were actually the beginning of labor. As I lay in bed, timing the rhythms of my body, it became clear that they were not going away. I woke up Dave to help me monitor what was happening. As we lay in bed, praying and thanking God for the miracle taking place, the contractions came closer and closer. What was even more miraculous was the fact that I went into labor on *this* day. Just 10 years earlier, I was having breakfast with my dad on the last morning I would wake up a single woman.

Every detail of the rest of the day could not have been planned more perfectly. We cleaned the house and got our oldest off to school; we even coached a CrossFit class (my husband, not me) in between contractions! After the class, we hopped in the car to get groceries, but quickly turned around to head to the hospital as the intensity made a quick shift to hard labor. A friend picked up our son Ben at the grocery store across from the hospital, and within the hour, we were in a delivery room readying to meet this new baby. Dave pulled out my phone to turn on worship music, and soon enough, the words of Lauren Daigle's song "Once And For All" filled the room as we heard the first cries of our beautiful baby girl, Beatrice Jane.

We both wept at the gift of this moment. Redeemed. In one moment, there was immediate reconciliation for this day I didn't know what to do with. The tears continued to flow as we realized that new life could exist alongside the first fragmented nine years we shared together. We didn't have to have one or the other; joy could hold hands with grief here, and it was beautiful. Our story was messy and complicated and painful... but it was still incredibly good. A beautiful reminder that God "works all things together for the good of those who love Him and are called according to His purpose." (Romans 8:28 ESV) April 15 was a reminder of all that He was doing and all He was yet to do.

A redeemed anniversary was a wonderful gift, a picture of the beauty that Jesus wants to bring from the ashes of failure. We felt a renewed sense of God's presence in even the smallest of details. We were growing into new people, with changed behavior and a common vision for our future together. We exposed the hidden and were working on creating a life characterized by authenticity and truth. Yet there still seemed to be something that was missing. We were hopeful, but not victorious. I couldn't quite put my finger on it, but despite all the joy I was experiencing, fear and confusion still played at the edges of my heart and mind.

Just one year removed from my husband's confession at the conference, I was still so bewildered as to how that had become our life. Somewhere deep inside me I knew that there was more for us, more work to be done. Staring out at the top of a glorious mountain peak, having summited the biggest challenge of our life together, I was beginning to realize that we would have to go back down and start up the next mountain. Our life wouldn't last long up on the heights of wonderful moments together but would blossom back down in the fruitful valley of wisdom and understanding. So, we began the descent back down.

# CHAPTER 16

# HOW DID WE GET HERE?

WHEN DAVE FIRST WENT BACK TO WORK, to traveling and spending most of his time away, the pain of betrayal was raw and fresh. It was like touching an open wound, searing so hot it could take your breath away. It was intense and exhausting, but it made me feel safe somehow—mostly because we were on the same side now, side by side, fighting anything that threatened our relationship.

As we moved further away from the moment the bright light exposed the truth in our marriage, paranoia silently took up residency in the back of my mind. We were a year and a half removed from the initial trauma of exposing his infidelity. While our game plan was still in place, the feeling of being on the front lines of an epic battle had diminished. The urgency of those first months had been dulled by the routine of life. We still had all the same security plans in place, guarding our marriage from outside invaders. I was increasingly afraid if we moved on from everything that had happened, if he let his guard down to even the smallest form of temptation, that I would have to live this whole tragedy again. I didn't think I could survive that.

By the time we reached "bye week" (a break with no game that each team has once in the season for a short respite), I was lost deep in a world of "what ifs" in my mind. Every small deviation from the extreme measures we were taking to protect our relationship felt like a sign that something was seriously wrong. If Dave didn't call me at the time he would normally call, or if he was distant and tired when he got home, I wondered what else he was thinking about or who he could possibly be talking to. However, I didn't want to address these fears because I was afraid of coming across as controlling or judgmental. I was living with the fallout of broken trust, but I didn't know how very real PTSD is for the betrayed. It is a dark, lonely, and deceptive place. I had no idea how to talk about what I was feeling and ask for help. My insecurities continued to grow, twisting my perception of reality. Underneath the newfound joy at our changing life together was a deep, lingering pain.

When those few precious days off came, we headed for the sanctuary of Glenwood. Instead of taking in the rugged beauty of the Cascade Mountains and the Yakima River Basin on the drive, I was haunted by the recent memory of all Dave had disclosed to me along this same road on our first trip after the marriage conference. With each mile, dread and uncertainty grew in the back of my mind. By the time we arrived at the quiet house, nothing but stars and trees surrounding us, I was exhausted from trying to block out the voices whispering inevitable doom. Completely unaware of my internal struggle and overcome by the exhaustion of midseason and travel, Dave collapsed into bed in relief. I quietly climbed in next to him after settling the kids in to sleep. As I tuned into his deep, rhythmic breathing, I almost willed myself to sleep, but I knew that if I pushed down my questions again, I might not find the courage or a window to ask him.

"Babe, can we talk for a minute?" I ventured quietly, almost hoping he was too deeply asleep to respond.

"Sure, what's up?" he sighed, rolling over toward me.

Staring up at the slatted ceiling, distancing myself from the vulnerability of facing him in my fear, I fumbled.

"Are you cheating on me again?"

A wave of heat crept up my face as I braced myself, trembling silently in the dark. I waited for his answer, an answer that I was almost certain was going to be the end of me.

"No," he responded flatly. "What makes you think that?" It was an ambush. In my right mind, I would have known better than to ask him that in the middle of the night, but indeed, my mind was *not* right. All the unhealed, unspoken emotional damage that comes with betrayal was eroding my sanity.

I don't really remember how I answered his question, but it didn't have much bearing in reality. I gave a number of reasons that seemed to make sense at the time. I could feel his body tensing away from me, the condemnation of my words furthering the space between us in the dark. He listened graciously, but I could sense his frustration growing as I tried to make sense of the battle I had been fighting in my mind.

"Babe, I don't really know what to tell you. I haven't had any interactions with women except the times there wasn't an option, and in those I have had, it's been professional." Like inviting someone to watch the final scene of a movie and asking them to understand the entire plot, he was confused and felt attacked. We were both dog-tired, and he knew nothing he was going to say was going to fix what I was feeling. While he was trying hard to understand me, his patience and understanding were as worn out as his body from months of minimal sleep.

In the silence that followed, he gave in to his exhaustion, but I lay awake for a while longer. I realized the insensitivity of my timing but also still felt justified for my concern. While my initial evidence trailed off into the oblivion of my endless fears, something deeper was trying to find a voice. I knew he was telling me the truth, but I didn't feel any better. As long as I was looking to his behavior to give me peace, I would be restless. Regardless of how much pain he had caused me, my healing wasn't his weight to carry. Even as his life changed and he grew into a new man, I needed to do my own work of inner healing. The answers would not be found in the present nor the uncertainty of the future. They lay in the past, in the wounds we had no idea how to access. Wounds that still needed to be uncovered and grace we still needed to receive. The scars were a roadmap, pointing us toward the next steps we needed to take to truly move into a healed and whole marriage.

Football season had wrapped up once again, and we were back to finding a rhythm together as a family. We were up early reading, spending evenings together, sharing the load of responsibility around the house, and heading to sports games and events as a whole crew. We seemed to be connected in a way that we never had before. Yet, in the middle of so much growth and good and new, there was a shadowy, dark presence that wouldn't disappear, no matter how hard I tried to ignore it. It was always looming just out of sight, and it was the question of *how*.

How in the world did we get to the desperate, dysfunctional, broken, lost place we found our marriage in almost two years ago? How did I continue to live that way, somehow knowing there was something deeply flawed, yet never saying anything?

I barely had time to acknowledge the lurking questions during football season. I had moments—usually late at night or when Dave was on the road—when I couldn't seem to escape the crushing menacing grip of dread. This usually led to conversations between us about specific instances of behavior that mimicked the past, but we never addressed the bigger questions formulating in my subconscious. Now that the season was over and life had slowed to a more manageable pace, I realized just how exhausted I was from carrying the questions in my head and heart.

My husband was charging forward into the new life we were creating, free from the bondage of hiding and shame, but I just couldn't shake the feeling that we were being followed.

We were running after the family we finally believed we could have, but I was beginning to see that we were also running away from the one we had before. The problem was, our old life wasn't going anywhere. No matter how much good I saw now, there was no light coming from the shadow of our past. And the further we got from there, the more clearly I saw how much landscape it covered.

You would think by now I would have trusted that having a hard conversation as soon as I realized it was needed was the best practice. But you have to remember that we had years of hiding things, sweeping them under the rug or pretending they weren't there, as muscle memory. We still mostly waited to dig into areas where we were disconnected when the break-down between us was affecting our daily interactions, and we couldn't ignore it anymore. We had changed some obviously destructive patterns, but it was becoming increasingly clear how deeply we had woven avoidance into the fabric of our marriage.

We had been to see a counselor early on when I was pregnant with Bea, but it was quickly apparent that her approach was just not right for us. We left her office feeling overwhelmed by how quickly she wanted to go to the darkness of our story with little connection or compassion for where we were starting. I'm sure some people really need that harsh reality check, but we had plenty of reality already. It didn't feel safe, and, at the time, safety was a top priority for both of us.

One of my dear friends, a woman who had lived through a similar situation as ours, told me about her experience with therapy. She spoke of the freedom it brought and how loved and seen she felt, and that was all I needed to know that it was time to try again. Sitting at the kitchen table one morning, bulletproof coffee in hand, I tested the waters.

"What do you think about seeing a counselor again?" I asked him. It seemed like a fair request, and I tried not to make it an accusation.

He took a long deep breath in, his hand reflexively reaching to rub his chin in thought. "I mean, I guess I just don't see the point. Therapy hasn't been around for very long, and as long as we have Jesus, I don't really know what it will do," he responded. I knew he was trying not to be defensive, but by the flare of his nostrils as he took a deep inhale, I could tell he was wrestling with the question. These were his honest, matter-of-fact feelings at the time.

I took a deep breath. I knew I had a choice to make. I could stick with what I knew, holding it together and finding the silver lining in this apparent dead end. Or, I could speak up and be open about what I needed and what I saw was possible, risking the vulnerability of my fragility.

"I know we have talked a lot about what went wrong, but I am wondering if we really understand how we got there. There is just so much I don't understand." I paused, searching for the right words. "I am really not doing well."

The words were out. I could feel my shoulders relax, finally having released carrying this weight in silence. "I want you to go to counseling with me if you will, but *I* have to go either way." The resolve in my words confirmed how my heart felt the second they left my mouth. It wasn't an ultimatum. I would have gone alone because it felt like the way forward. There wasn't much else to say. We were on a different page and arguing wasn't going to help. He said he would think and pray about it.

The next day, during our daily lunchtime check-in, he totally surprised me. "I called the counselor. We talked for about 10 minutes. I briefly told him our story, and he said he wanted to meet with us. We have an appointment on Sunday night if that works for our schedule?"

I was floored. Shocked by this sudden switch, I asked, "What made you change your mind?"

"I prayed about it, and I felt like God was telling me that, as long as this guy is basing his knowledge in the Bible and really is a believer, it isn't going to hurt anything. I think we should go and just see what he is about."

I held the phone to my ear for a minute before I found the words. "Thank you, Babe. This feels really good to me." A wave of relief mingled with a tinge of fear passed through my body. I knew we had crossed yet another threshold in this journey toward new life.

We had no idea what we were opening ourselves up to, but we were going together, and that was a great place to start. With trepidation, we took the next step in the direction of healing. Little did we know that this small decision would open a door into a wide-open country we had never known before. The result would not always make life easier; in fact, it did quite the opposite in many ways. Nevertheless, it would take us to places we had never imagined.

———— ✦ ————

Dave: "David, you ~~are doing a good job of narrating what hap-~~ pened, but you are telling the story as if you were not there," said our counselor, a 70-year-old man with a strong build, a silver flat-top, and the biggest gap-toothed smile. Sitting in his tiny office with the peaceful sound of his desktop fountain gurgling in the background, I felt stuck. Like most men, I felt at a loss for words. I learned that there is actually a name for this: alexithymia. Simply put, it is an inability to put your feelings into words. I felt as if I were having one of those nightmares where you try to scream for help, but your voice box doesn't seem to work. All I knew was that I felt stuck in my past with no tools to get me out of there.

Imagine a digital geography map with red pins on it that represent traumatic experiences from your past. Then, imagine that just above each of these points on the map is an icon of a key or lock. The experiences you have fully felt and dealt with have the key icon hovering over the top of the red pin. The experiences that you have just moved on from and forgotten, on the other hand, have the lock icon hovering over the top of it.

Let me clarify: When I say you've "dealt with" these traumatic experiences, I don't necessarily mean that you have a full understanding of what happened; I just mean that you have at least looked at it from a different perspective, with new information, and remember what it is you felt at that time. The saying "history repeats itself" comes to mind—any problem we failed to deal with properly will emerge again in a different way later on in our lives.

My problem was that up to this point, I had no desire to even acknowledge how important an emotional map was, let alone address the red pins of trauma waiting to be dealt with. As a man, I wasn't taught to connect with my emotions. Many men aren't. When Lizzy approached me about going to counseling, I gave her a hundred reasons why we didn't need it, when all I was actually doing was trying to avoid the work it would take to recover from the trauma of my past.

I was committed to changing my behavior, morally speaking, but I could not see the importance of looking into the past to connect the dots to see how I came to this place. Lizzy could see that I was committed to changing my ways, but sensing that there was another growth step coming for me, she brought up the inevitable.

"It seems like you are doing really well, but you had some seriously bad habits. Aren't you curious about how you got there?" I hated it when she would bring that up. Truth be told, I don't handle being bad at much of anything, and I definitely didn't want to be exposed for my lack of emotional intelligence. In any case, I knew where her comments were heading, and I knew she wanted to go to counseling.

The night before, after mentioning that she would go without me, I knew I had a decision to make. I decided to go with her because I was committed to restoring our marriage. Little did I know that it had less to do with our relationship and way more to do with my own psychological and emotional wellbeing. In my mind, I had pictured counseling as the two of us sitting side by side, scrutinizing our marriage together. I imagined it to be very clinical, just narrating the story of our marriage from our own perspective and assessing the issues we've run into along the way. But after our first session, feeling completely drained by the emotional heavy lifting that took place, I could sense that I was very wrong about my assumption. It was humbling to find out that I was exercising a muscle that was very weak.

I remember one of our weekly sessions about a month in that shook me to my core and made me realize that I desperately needed help. Lizzy was talking about how betrayal had made her feel when I noticed our counselor looking at me. He gently stopped Lizzy and asked me, "David, I want you to look at Liz. What do you think she is feeling?"

I turned to look at Lizzy, studied her face for a few seconds, and said, "She's sad and hurt."

With his lips pursed together, he tilted his head to the side, and said to Lizzy, "Liz, you are angry, aren't you?" She started sobbing even harder and nodded, unable to speak through the tears.

It's hard for me to admit that my initial reaction to Lizzy's emotional breakdown was embarrassment that I answered wrong. My selfish inner critic immediately brought a wave of shame in an attempt to keep me from seeing Lizzy in this moment. But before I could go into defense mode and try to explain my response away to protect myself, I was overwhelmed by a deep sadness for her. I realized that I was trying to control her emotional responses in our relationship. I saw her sadness as an acceptable emotion because it seemed more submissive and didn't require any further action by me other than comfort. Anger, on the other hand, meant that I couldn't just hug her or sweet talk her into a better emotional state. Anger required a different set of skills to resolve, skills that I did not possess at the time. Even writing the last two sentences feels indicative of the fact that I thought it was my responsibility to help her to cope with her emotions. As hard as this was for me, I knew I was in the right place. It was uncharted territory, but I had a great guide in our counselor.

After that session, Lizzy and I went for a walk along Lake Washington, conveniently across the street from the counseling office. It was a beautiful spring evening in Kirkland. There was hardly anyone at the park we walked to, and it was the perfect setting for us to process the session we had just left. Lizzy, in a very loving but straightforward way, unloaded years of resentment on me. I remember her saying, "I have felt so unseen and unheard by you. I feel like you have never given me permission to feel any of the pain you have caused. As soon as I want to talk about something hard, you want to move forward to what is next." It made so much sense. As I listened to her process, I was struck by the truth in her words. It all started to make sense as I really heard her—perhaps for one of the first times in our marriage.

"I am so sorry," I said, unable to say much else. My mind felt scrambled, kind of like the empty, lightheaded feeling you get after taking one of those long tests like the SAT or ACT. All I could do was listen.

Then, something astounding started to happen. I realized that as we were walking and talking, I began to notice micro-changes in her facial expressions. It was as if I were on an emotional roller coaster *with* her. When she felt sad, I noticed and began to feel sad with her. When she felt angry, I noticed and began to feel her anger and accept that I was the one who had caused it. When she felt compassion toward me because of my sadness, I felt loved. I realized that I was exercising a new muscle called empathy, and like trying any new type of exercise, it was exhausting.

As stressful as that counseling session was, I felt a deep sense of peace and compassion, not only for Lizzy but for myself as well. The problems in our marriage—and especially in my personal life—were starting to make sense to me. I had been purposely ignoring emotional cues my entire life. To me, emotions showed weakness, distracted me from achieving my personal goals, and represented a place where I was severely deficient. Emotions attacked the masculine identity I had formed for myself up to that point in my life. But now, with these new tools, I felt a sense of hope that I could make more sense of my true identity.

I found my emotional map that day, and I had been given a key to start unlocking all those red pins.

——— ❖ ———

Lizzy: Going to counseling was an invaluable gift to our marriage. What I gained was truly surprising. I thought we would go and learn why we had been able to live in our fractured relationship without feeling any urgency to confront it. What I gained instead were tools to understand myself. I thought what I needed most was for Dave to see me, and that was helpful for sure, but by far the most important skill I developed was learning to see myself. When the counselor looked at my face and named the emotion *anger*, it was as if the floodgates were opened to a deep emotional reservoir. I could finally feel and name what I was experiencing.

How could I even imagine I would be able to fully participate in my marriage when I wasn't able to make the connections for myself? I could feel the physical symptoms of the emotions, but I usually managed them with control or anger, often internalizing my seething resentment and distancing myself from my husband. It was risky and vulnerable to expose what was really happening under my anger. As I learned to connect with my sadness and my hidden shame, I felt alive and present in a way that I never had before. Instead of feeling disconnected from my heart and my thoughts, I was able to bring more of me to our relationship. I finally felt fully known.

## CHAPTER 17

# THE NEXT RIGHT STEP

THERE ARE SO MANY MORE STORIES that we could tell of all that has transpired in our relationship since we finally stopped hiding from the truth and each other. With every step we take toward each other and the truth, our marriage just keeps getting deeper and richer. But now it's your turn. You have a decision to make. You picked up this book for a reason or someone gave it to you because they believed you needed to read it. Whatever brought you to this point, this is where our story stops, and your story begins. The following pages contain insights on what worked for us, for finding our way into the joy of a great marriage, with suggestions of what we know worked for us. These are a starting point for you.

For those of you who are not ready to dig in, to confront whatever is standing in the way of your great marriage, the book ends here. You cannot go further if you aren't willing to be totally honest and expose the true you. It will take time and it will take a concerted effort to keep coming back to your wounds. Somewhere underneath your false self is the person you were always meant to become. The only prerequisite for the rest of this life-changing adventure is a commitment to transparency and vulnerability, a willingness to confess and confront hard truths as they come up.

We hope that reading our story has helped you in one way or another. At a minimum, you may feel better about the current struggles you are having in your relationship because at least you are not alone. However, we did not write this book to make anyone feel good about the common battles that exist in marriage. In fact, the only thing that makes us qualified to say anything at all is that we are living proof that telling the hard, scary truths to each other is the only way to find a truly great relationship.

So, where do you begin? It's not complicated. But it's likely one of the hardest things you'll ever do. It's not all that mysterious or grand. It's small and doesn't move you very far, but over the course of a lifetime, it will make all the difference. David Whyte says, "Take the next right step, the one closest in, the one you don't want to take."

We're guessing that you probably know the next step without having to dig very deep. Maybe you need to admit something you've been hiding. Maybe you need to share something that is hurting you, but you've felt afraid to say anything. Maybe you just need to ask an honest question of yourself, or you need to decide to be the first one to go see a counselor. There is no secret formula or magical pathway to a better marriage; you just have to be willing to take the first step toward the marriage you want. Then, take another step, followed by the next one after that. If you don't move toward it now, it will be waiting for you down the road when you have to stop running again to take a breath.

Lying there in the dark, scared and lonely, we were lost. How could we have known that one question would begin a chain reaction, and everything would change? "This marriage?" was simply a response to take the next right step—to tell the truth of where we were that night. Leaving the comfort of self-protection, we stopped trying to survive in our relationship and began the quest to thrive. There have been many deep valleys, times we wondered if we would ever leave the swamp. There have also been incredible peaks, the sheer magnitude of what is out there to explore overwhelming us as we reach the summit of some of our biggest victories. The depth of intimacy we share is something we only ever dreamed of, and yet we know this is only the beginning.

Take away the question mark and replace it with a period. *This marriage.* A statement instead of a hesitation. A place we have come to trust where we can do the hardest work because of our foundation of authentic vulnerability and forgiveness.

Are you ready to find out what yours can become? Take the step. We promise it will be worth it.

# CHAPTER 18

# PERSONAL INVENTORY

AFTER YOU LOCATE what you are feeling in your marriage, it is time to start digging into why you are feeling this way. Here is where you tell the truth about yourself, to yourself. Up to this point, you may have been content with the status quo, willing to keep your own struggles private so you don't rock the boat. You may not have some big lie to cover up, but it could be as simple as an unwillingness to be honest about your discontentment or a resignation to just lead separate emotional lives. Something is keeping you from the life you were meant to live together, and now is the time to be honest.

You may want to go someplace by yourself or start a confidential journal until you've gained the courage to share it with your spouse or a confidant. We want you to remember one thing: There is so much grace for you here, more than you know.

———— ✦ ————

Dave: When I was still going out, partying on the road, a fellow coach gently called me out on my waywardness. At the time I wasn't ready to receive his words, but now I understand and value what he was getting at. Sherman came into my office one day and asked me "Dave, you were a quarterback. Do you ever throw interceptions on purpose?"

Obviously, my answer was no, but he wasn't finished. "Then why are you out there trying to throw interceptions?" He was challenging who I was claiming to be and the choices I was making in the dark, asking me to be honest with myself about how I was really living.

Lizzy was sure something was wrong with our marriage, and she was right. I had a few serious problems that she didn't know about. My struggles were easy to identify but extremely difficult to confess. I knew it was going to require some very humbling truth-telling on my part and a lot of grace from Lizzy if we were going to make it. It was such a risky endeavor on both of our parts. Lizzy called out our broken marriage and I made some pretty dark confessions: I needed to stop pursuing sex outside of my marriage and I needed to stop drinking as much as I was.

The work did not stop there. The more difficult changes happened in the truly private places of my life that no one knew about. A huge part in the severed intimacy that I was experiencing with Lizzy was because I was addicted to pornography. It was like a "gateway drug" for me, creating pathways in my brain that allowed me to use sex coldly for my own benefit. It was a secret, silent struggle that I had years before I was married, and one that is advertised as not really a problem, even considered a normal part of being a man. I needed to separate myself from anything in my life that was working against Lizzy and I having a great marriage.

As I gained the courage to take a truthful look at all areas of my life, I felt like I was constantly putting out small fires. The minute I felt like I was gaining ground on one problem, another one would show up. I realized I needed a way to systemize my self-evaluation so that I could start living proactively, pursuing my best, instead of living reactively, just trying to keep my head above water. It felt like such a daunting task to keep a complete inventory of all the areas of my life.

One day as I was strategizing about my life with my friend Jason, he had a truly brilliant idea. He said, "You make playbooks for a living. Why don't you and Lizzy make one for your marriage?" What he meant was this: Make a plan for the areas in your life that you know present opportunities for behavior that has a negative impact on your relationship with your wife. I had a lot of secret places where, practically speaking, my wife was not there, and I could get away with whatever I wanted. Knowing that my wife is affected whether she knows what I am doing or not was very helpful. I needed to put protections around those places by being honest with myself and creating boundaries, so I wasn't constantly being tempted.

Some practical steps in our playbook that keep me from temptation are blocking movie-ordering capabilities in my hotel room, staying in my hotel at night, and avoiding the hotel lobby after team meetings. I no longer have any business being in a bar with a group of friends, and for sure not without my wife. I quit drinking alcohol altogether, knowing that I do not have great restraint in that area, and it numbs me to making other poor choices. I keep my interactions with other women brief and professional, and I don't put myself in situations where I will be alone with a female. If I have to text or email another woman, I include my wife in the interaction. This is not to have her monitor the interaction, but to set a precedent that whatever I am doing is transparent. These decisions may seem extreme, but the autonomy I am sacrificing is well worth what it creates between Lizzy and me: trust.

Having the courage to take an honest look at myself in the mirror has been life-giving. What I learned was that the only way to be truly grounded is to be 100% honest with your shortcomings. That is exactly what I did. I grew comfortable looking at the things that used to bring me so much shame. When I started to see myself the way God sees me, I was no longer ashamed. I felt compassion for a man who was broken, realizing that I was incapable of growing into the man God intended me to be as long as I was trying to fix the problems myself. I felt Him calling me to something greater, and I finally started to want that for myself.

———— ❖ ————

Lizzy: When I first really admitted to myself that our marriage was not where I wanted it to be, I wanted it to be my husband's fault. I wanted it to be because of his choices and for him to take all the blame. I didn't want to take an inventory of my own personal brokenness because it would mean I would have to relinquish the security I felt in trying to control the chaos outside, instead of turning my attention to my inner turmoil. I was terrified of what I might find if I dug deeper than the hurt of my betrayal.

The truth for me was that I was struggling with deep personal shame. My shame came from a deep fear that I wasn't actually doing a good job of being a grown-up, wife, and mother. Having it all together was what I hung my hat on. It's how popular culture assigns value. Success, beauty, and control are all indicators that we are enough, especially as moms and wives. I was terrified to dig into why I felt like a disappointment, a failure. It was a lot easier to make it someone else's problem and to try to control the image I was projecting to the rest of the world.

I was well aware of the perception people often have that my family lives a charmed life. Subconsciously, I kept expecting that, as we climbed up the success ladder, how I felt about myself would catch up to what people saw on the outside. The burden of perceived expectation that I should have it all together, especially because we have found worldly success, weighed heavily on me. For so long, I feared being seen as a failure if I didn't make it look like an effortless endeavor to carry my family through the ebbs and flows of football life. The flicker of awe I still see cross people's faces when they learn I'm married to a professional football coach reminds me of how tempted we all are by fame, fortune, relevance, and comfort. In a strange way, one of the greatest gifts to come from our crisis was being forced to stop the charade. My pain made it impossible to be anything but who I was.

One of the first decisions I made was to stop listening to what the rest of the world said was valuable. I canceled all of my social media accounts, extracting myself from the fight for relevance and the constant dopamine hit of *likes* and *shares*. I thought it would be for a season, and I soon realized that those tools were robbing me of joy, making me feel inferior, and keeping me from the relationships that were right in front of me. It requires more effort to stay connected to the people I love and, to be honest, many people have fallen away. I also realized that the quantity of friendships was no substitute for a few quality relationships. Scrolling down feeds and posts made me feel like I was connected, but it was just a replacement for the real work of loving people in genuine community.

The other thing I had to do was to learn to turn toward my husband in my hurt and fear, offering only what was happening inside me, instead of hiding and punishing him by disengaging from our relationship. I had to stop seeking relief from our problems and instead seek restoration through truthful conversations. I had to be willing to be vulnerable with my own heart instead of blaming him and harboring resentment. I didn't need to wait until I had the perfect, airtight argument to justify what I was feeling. I was allowed to be unraveled without needing to prove that my feelings were warranted.

The reality is that marriage, raising families, and engaging in meaningful work is challenging for everyone, regardless of the details of your specific life and calling. Add in the crazy challenge of living through a global pandemic, financial instability, and any kind of emotional or physical trauma, and none of us are able to hold it all together. Eventually, something will have to give, no matter how strong or practiced you are at making it look like everything is OK. The freedom I found during this incredibly painful season of life is something I think most of us crave: the chance to be unapologetically right here. On the days I just can't juggle everything, I have found true freedom in not pretending I can.

I can be exhausted, I can mess it all up, I can take my frustration out on my kids, I can admit my weaknesses and vulnerabilities, and I can ask for help. I know that I am enough because I am loved by God. In the midst of my failure, when we were living our life so backward and not asking for any guidance, I have also seen that God was able to weave those events into a beautiful story that has brought us up and out of a *very* dark pit. If you are feeling exhausted, hopeless, and afraid that there is no way out, take heart.

In death, Jesus brought life forever—abundant life that can never run dry. In giving up your need to be in control, He can create the most unbelievable miracles from the ashes of any self-protecting and self-promoting schemes. Let go of what you thought it was *supposed* to be, to what you always envisioned it would look like, and just be honest with where you are *right now*. Trust me, He can work with that.

# CHAPTER 19

# INVITE PEOPLE IN

LIKE A SNEAKY LITTLE MINION, perception had a grip on Dave and me before we were ever married. Once we had a home together, it moved in and got really comfortable. Hiding behind the assumptions that threatened to keep us silent and locked away in our separate dungeons of isolation, it whispered threats of losing everything. We avoided exposure of our frailty, painting an attractive picture for the outside world—one that we even believed most of the time. It had us right where it wanted us, stuck in what we *should* be, afraid of letting anyone in. We had made an agreement with the lie that it wasn't safe to be broken or to not know what to do next. We were tragically unprepared to have an authentic, profound relationship. Although desperate to get out from the stony grasp of living a lie, we felt helpless to do anything but pretend.

And then the truth came in like a cool, refreshing breeze on a sweltering day. "Even if you lose everything, you will still have Me. I will never leave you." The promise was like oxygen, seeping into every corner of our life. Finally, we were ready to open the doors and let in the spring. Freedom began with one jarring question from a desperate wife after another lonely night. Brick by brick, the fortress walls crumbled, each question pushing us one more step toward the adventure of a lifetime. With the light flooding in and the breeze blowing through, we saw this agent of darkness for what it really was: a weak, sniveling lie that only had power because we thought it did. It had to flee.

After the marriage conference, the change in the climate of our house was immediate. Not only were we free from the grasp of the lie, but pretending we had it all together was no longer an option. Starting with friends who had also attended the marriage conference, we began inviting people into the midst of our suffering and asking for help. In the early days, we didn't have many answers, just a painfully honest look into our own situation. Our friendships began to transform as we shared our story with the people we loved. With each new telling, we began to realize an amazing truth: People didn't want answers to their problems. They didn't want friends who had a perfect life. They wanted somewhere to be messed up, too. In sharing our brokenness, we created a haven for people to take an honest inventory. Just like us, they wanted to be seen and heard and feel safe to admit that life is hard.

I will never forget the beautiful way living authentically changed the pleasant but light relationship we had with our friends Josh and Jenn. We barbecued, went to each other's kids' birthday parties, and even vacationed together before the transformation of our marriage; but we never really scratched the surface of true friendship. When their daughter was diagnosed with type 1 diabetes, their world was suddenly rocked with the weight of their frightening new reality. They opened up to us about their fear and struggle, and we walked alongside them before we started doing that work for ourselves.

One summer night, they invited us over for dinner, and we knew we had to tell them the truth of what was happening in our home. We fumbled through the story as my husband unraveled the picture we had created for them over the years. Their response was unbelievably gracious and loving and their support overwhelming. It transformed our relationship. We still love to have fun together, but now we dive right into whatever is really happening first. We've invited each other into struggles with anxiety, difficulty in family relationships, and parenting and marital struggles. When I am having a hard day, one of the safest places I can go is to Jenn's couch, curled under a blanket with a fresh cup of coffee.

Telling the truth has transformed all my relationships. I was always close with my younger sister and mom, but now we are learning to do the hard work we've been needing for years. Each time we press into conflict and have conversations about the ways we hurt each other, we come out healthier and more connected. I asked a few challenging, honest questions of a fellow mom I met at the beach park as we were first getting to know each other, and we quickly became confidants. Our weekly hill walks taught me how to bare my soul to another woman, and to pursue truth together. There is nothing that compares to the security of being seen and loved by people that really know you.

Another dear friend, a seasoned coach's wife, paid me the ultimate compliment the last time she was at my house. "I just love coming here," she said as we were gathering coffee cups at the end of one of our coaches' and players' Bible study. "I'm so glad you are hosting because it is just so normal. It's lived in and messy, and people can come and just *be* here." In what feels like another lifetime ago, I might have been offended as she called my house "normal," but instead, I heard her say "safe."

The more we invite people to know about God's miraculous rescue of our life, the more we have to stop and take an inventory of ourselves again. This beautiful cycle keeps us honest, never settling into a new complacent normal, challenging us to continue to prune and nurture the work in our marriage.

We have a picture in our living room of a man standing at the door to a lighthouse. Just as the photo was taken, a huge wave crashed around the building behind him, threatening to sweep him away in the fury of the storm. The story behind the photo is that he was outside looking for the rescue helicopter coming to take him to freedom. He ducked back inside the building only to be safely flown to shore a few minutes later. All of us will face a storm that we cannot wait out—one that we must be rescued from. By sharing the truth of our story, our deep desire now is to offer hope to other people when the tempest breaks. We hid too long in a crumbling lighthouse, trying to be a beacon of hope when we were in imminent danger of being swept out to sea. How sweet it is to be on the helicopter now, searching for people who need to know of their true rescue, just waiting for them to peek out long enough to know God is just waiting to take them to a better place.

———— ❖ ————

Dave: Sharing my story with people led to some deeper friendships than I'd ever had. While I was willing to share it with anyone, there were only a few men who went to the depths with me and heard my true heart's desire. It stirred their hearts as they were looking for deeper, more meaningful marriages and connections with likeminded people.

It didn't take me long to realize that it was God who had placed two men on the Seahawks staff whom I admired greatly. Sherman Smith and Rocky Seto are true disciples of Jesus Christ. Both of them embody the kind of man I want to be, and it feels as if God placed them in my life to allow me to get a glimpse of what I can become if I truly let the Holy Spirit transform me.

Knowing that they genuinely cared about me is what gave me the courage to be vulnerable with them about my struggles. I could tell they cared because they told me the truth even though they knew I didn't want to hear it. I needed that kind of tough love in my life. I met with them in their offices and asked them for forgiveness. I apologized for trying to make them think I was a perfectly put-together Christian while hiding my personal problems. Then, I told them the truth about who I was and the depth of what I was walking through. Just as they took a risk to get involved in my life, I took a risk by letting them in. Thankfully, each man embraced me with open arms. Where I expected shame and judgment, I received the grace and love of Jesus. They were genuinely excited about my decision to walk with Jesus and assured me of their full commitment to walk alongside me.

My friends, Josh, Ben, and Rocky rallied to me, feeling my desperation for change. We went to the scriptures together via text message, and got on weekly phone calls early in the morning to match my crazy schedule. We also spent time together when traveling for road games together, helping me establish new routines and habits that have lasted for years.

My two biological brothers, Josh and Coba, spent precious time and money to fly to road games around the country and spend time with me while I reordered my life. I can't express the love and support I felt from them as I was finding my way. My cousin-in-law Kevin made time in his schedule weekly to check in on me and ask me the hard questions that I didn't want to answer. He knew I needed to be reminded what was at stake and wanted me to know that he loved me.

My circles kept growing as I saw how gratifying authentic brotherhood was. I shared my story with people who had known one version of me or the other, some of whom I'd been friends with for a long time. There were people who turned away from me for sure, the cold hard truth of who

I had been hiding either so offensive or convicting it was too hard to maintain a surface-level relationship. Some people were hurt that I pretended to be a good Christian guy. They felt lied to and betrayed. It has taken years to mend some of those friendships, and some of them we've never regained. Other people acted happy for us in the moment, but suddenly stopped calling because either they felt awkward getting into our personal lives or because it brought up shame in theirs.

But far more friends were all in, ready to dive into the depths of true authenticity. My life has become so full because of these loyal and encouraging people. We were often surprised at the wisdom and perspective that many of our friends offered us—perspective that we would have never known about had we not opened up to them. We were especially encouraged by a few couples and individuals who had similar stories. Their feedback was like gold to us.

All of these relationships grew because I was willing to make myself vulnerable and they were willing to get messy with me as I faced my battles. That's the secret sauce to great relationships. *That* is real love. Identifying your circle of people is critical to your growth. I would challenge you to look around and identify the people you admire and would like to go deeper with. Start with those closest to you and work your way outward.

If you really want to get to know someone better, then you have to be willing to share your story. Don't let fear of rejection or exposure keep you from the blessing of deep and meaningful relationships. We were not meant to do this life alone.

In fact, isolation is one of the greatest weapons against us because when we are alone, we can easily believe lies. Surround yourself with truth-tellers who are deeply connected to you because they know your story, and you know theirs.

I would encourage you to pray and ask God to show you who these people are. Go to them humbly and with an open heart to both receive and give whatever God has for you. I truly believe that you will find people who are more than willing to share their life experiences with you. Maybe more importantly, they will model for you what it looks like to disciple others that will seek *you* out someday, just like Sherm and Rocky did for me.

I believe that God has tailor-made specific people to pour into your life (and for you to pour into theirs) during challenging seasons. These people have experience you can learn from—oftentimes experience your parents can't offer. And you have experience for others that only *you* can offer. The only way to find them is by being willing to tell your story whenever and wherever your story needs to be heard.

## CHAPTER 20

# GET HELP, GATHER WISDOM

JEREMIAH 6:16: "This is what the Lord says; 'Stand at the crossroads and look; ask for the ancient paths, ask where the good way is and walk in it, and you will find rest for your souls.'"

Eventually you'll reach the end of your personal inventory and find that you don't really know what to do next. The people you've invited into your work will be really wonderful and supportive, but they will not have all of the answers. You will have to make yourself vulnerable again and keep pursuing healing when you get stuck.

The good news is, there is help out there. We cannot say it enough times: Go. To. Counseling. There are people who have spent their lives studying, learning, understanding, and mastering the connections between what we do and why. They have done the work that you probably don't even know how to start, and they can lead you to the treasure of your own *why*.

They understand how the brain works, how to get to the heart of what is really going on, and practical steps to take to move you away from dysfunctional habits and patterns. They can literally help you rewrite the script of your life. The scariest part of going to counseling for us was making the phone call and getting through the door.

There are some qualified, wonderful counselors who cannot wait to help you navigate your emotional world. In our experience, our counselor was willing to go at our pace. He could sense when enough was enough, and he never pushed us to dig further than we were willing or able. A good counselor does not aim to make you feel badly; they simply act as a mirror of your emotions so you can see the truth of what you are feeling inside. By connecting with us, our counselor was modeling what healthy emotional connection looked like as well. Here is some of what we learned about ourselves.

———— ❖ ————

Dave: Becoming emotionally aware has been the greatest challenge of my life. Looking back, I can see the wake of damage I left in my relationships because I was unwilling (and mostly incapable) of seeing what I was doing to the people around me. When I was a young, single man, my dysfunction did not feel as urgent or as costly. I could mostly ignore my flaws, deceiving myself that I was living a successful life. But nothing exposes your deficiencies more than being married and having children. Your family is a mirror showing you the truth of your emotional wellbeing, if you are willing to look at them long enough to see.

I am sure you know what it is like to be misunderstood emotionally. You feel unseen and unimportant. Being seen is one of the most basic human needs. Right up there with food and shelter, being seen means you belong and ensures your survival. Destructive behavior is often directly connected to people feeling invisible or isolated, and is often a cry for attention. I was sabotaging my personal life in part because I didn't feel seen or heard or important enough. I was trying to fill that emotional void with pseudo-intimate experiences, not knowing how to pursue the genuine relationships I really wanted.

I've learned how to enter into conversations with my hands down so that I'm not automatically in a defensive posture, trying to protect my identity. I still really struggle with being wrong. Success can be defined many different ways depending on what your family or community celebrates. In my family, we valued spirituality, education, and athletics, which is what we were celebrated for the most. In my case, I did not measure up to my brothers when it came to these metrics. I was semi-interested in church happenings, never a straight "A" student, and I was an above-average athlete. I had some special moments of achievement, but they were exceptions and not the rule. Because of this, I always felt like I had to do something spectacular to be important.

It took me a long time to realize that the most important thing is to be true to the passions in my heart. God makes us all different. It takes all kinds of people to make up a tribe. We can't all be the star and we can't all be the supporting staff. I know now that my special qualities are in bringing people together and creating deep connections. I always thought I had to be the best of the best, when all I had to be was me.

Growing in emotional intelligence has helped me to be more truthful in the way that I look at myself and given me space to recognize my insecurities. It has been very powerful to acknowledge that I am high on the narcissistic spectrum. I like to joke about the fact that I am a recovering narcissist. I have had to work very hard at developing the skills necessary to be aware beyond myself and my needs. I'm a verbal processor and have talked for most of my marriage, but I've had a lot of help learning how to ask generous questions.

———— ◈ ————

Lizzy: To be totally transparent, I've done a better job of being gracious with broken people *outside* our family than I have with the ones right under our own roof. In the years since Dave and I reconciled, it saddens me to think about how, in the upheaval of my world, I fought for control of my children. Instead of admitting that I was helpless and at the mercy of this process, I tried to make sure that they didn't behave in any way that mimicked our brokenness. I was so distracted with my own pain. When I would finally stop moving long enough to feel it, it was debilitating. Then

I would snap back into reality to correct and control my kids, speaking to them in ways I would never speak to someone else, not even my husband. I was asking them to make my life feel better by being obedient and easy, in an attempt to calm my internal chaos.

That is a weight too heavy to bear for anyone, especially a child.

I am realizing that I have a hard time attuning to my children's needs when they get overwhelmed because I don't know how to do that well for myself. I am still learning that I don't have to be unbreakable.

For me, counseling was first and foremost a safe place for me to deal with the trauma of betrayal and the place where I learned to hear my own heart. I didn't struggle to hear my own voice, for I was always confident in my decisions and abilities. Where I needed help was connecting to my emotions and believing that they were important, not another thing to control. Instead of entering into my marriage with what I have to give, I can bring who I am.

When I am hurting, I can stop and ask myself what is really going on instead of punishing anyone else with my overwhelming feelings. Grace for myself becomes grace for my family. Nothing compares to the joy I feel when I hear my kids apologize to each other on their own after an offense. I have hope knowing they are learning to bring their brokenness to each other to be reconciled. We still don't have it all figured out, and we are never going to arrive at a magical place where we no longer have to work at our relationships.

But with each failure, we can honestly come together to find restoration and healing. My kids just want to know that even in their mess, they are safe and loved. Finding that certainty for myself first, then bringing that into my marriage is now transforming my family.

Another way that we continue to pursue growth is through reading together. Each off season we pick a few books to read during our morning coffee. We are intentional about getting up before our kids and having time to learn together. Dave reads out loud while I listen, and then we process what we are hearing. The books change as our needs change. Reading these books is like a tune-up, constantly checking in with how we are doing and creating space to learn tools and wisdom that will help us keep growing.

There are incredibly intelligent people who have spent their life's energy studying specific areas, gaining insight that they present in bite-sized actionable format, making it easy and accessible for people like us. Instead of finding our way to the answers we need, we are asking these experts for their wisdom. We read books about marriage, healing masculinity and femininity, healing sexual trauma and healthy intimacy, holistic health and nutrition, parenting, psychology, and neurological science. Each of these deepens our understanding of ourselves in an area we lack. We have included a list of the books at the back of the book that we recommend that have been invaluable to the development of a thriving marriage, cultivating individual identity, and overall wellness.

One of the books we read, *The Road Back to You*, by Suzanne Stabile and Ian Morgan Cron, introduced us to another tool that has transformed our relationship: the Enneagram. This personality typing is of unknown origin, dating possibly back to the early Christian monastic tradition. It has been studied and developed over centuries, gaining popularity in the 20th century in Christian and secular circles. "The Enneagram teaches that there are nine different personality styles in the world, one of which we naturally gravitate toward and adopt in childhood to cope and feel safe. Each type or number has a distinct way of seeing the world and an underlying motivation that powerfully influences how that type thinks, feels and behaves."[1] In short, the Enneagram has helped us understand how our personalities are a gift that served us in surviving our early lives, but can take us quickly into self-protection and disconnection.

Dave is a type 3, the performer: "success-oriented, image conscious and wired for productivity, they are motivated by a need to be (or appear to be) successful and avoid failure."[2] I am a type 7, the enthusiast: "fun, spontaneous and adventurous, they are motivated by the need to be happy, to plan stimulating experiences and to avoid pain."[3] Even just the description gives us a deeper insight into why we've struggled. There are countless ways understanding our motivations has

1  Cron, 2016, pg.24
2  Cron, 2016, pg. 26
3  Cron, 2016, pg. 26

led to deeper connection between the two of us. Instead of feeling shame for our self-protective ways, we often laugh now when one of us catches ourselves fully immersed in our own number. These personality types are not a self-fulfilling excuse to act a certain way, but instead a tool to help us understand why and get unstuck.

We have coffee mugs that describe us perfectly. "That's a horrible idea. What time?" makes me chuckle because it is so true, but also reminds me that I don't have to run from the parts of my life that are hard, and that I don't like. Often, that is where my best work and deepest growth comes from. Dave's mug says, "Living the dream, while chasing the next." While progress and achievement are worthwhile goals, they can easily distract him from being present right here and hide when he doesn't feel like he is performing well. The Enneagram is a powerful tool that you can add to your arsenal for fighting for your marriage.

The point is this: Seek help wherever you can find it. You don't have to stay in your limited understanding of yourself or your struggles. The Bible makes it clear in Proverbs 4:7, "Sell everything and buy Wisdom! Forage or understanding." (The Message Translation) The beauty of community is perspective. Expand your community to include experts, in whatever form you can get, and expand your understanding of yourself, your struggles, and your relationships. Truth and insight will not disappoint you on this journey toward wholeness.

# CHAPTER 21

# IT'S ALWAYS THE RIGHT TIME

IT'S NEVER THE RIGHT TIME; it's always the right time.

This has become a mantra in our home—the declaration Dave and I try to embody when dealing with whatever comes up between us. It is never going to be easy or feel like perfect timing to uncover how we offend each other, so we try to talk about whatever we are struggling with as soon as we can. It used to take us weeks, months, and, in many cases, years to bring up hard conversations. Usually, we avoided them and found a workaround in the form of a fun date, a family vacation, or even a few shots over ice. We were even skilled at talking *around* an issue to give us the sense that we had faced it. But the truth is, avoidance only ever delayed the inevitability that the same issue would show up somewhere else. Like a giant game of whack-a-mole at the fair, we kept trying to pop those little arguments back underground instead of just calling an exterminator.

It is a practice that has taken much trial and error to shift from avoidance to authentic vulnerability. It requires offering up your own pain and failure to your partner for a chance at finding a better solution. Most of the time, we still make a mess of it, clumsily running into each other with harsh accusations and defensive responses, followed by humble apologies. Still, our response time is quicker, and with a shorter interval between offense and resolution, the damage of each violation is diminished. Moving toward each other when we are offended is a muscle that needs to be exercised over and over to become a reflex, gaining strength each time we use it.

We really got to put this muscle to work navigating our new normal during the restrictions of the global pandemic.

Seattle was the epicenter of the first outbreak of COVID-19 cases in the country. In an effort to slow the spread of the virus, the governor enacted stay-at-home orders, mandating all non-essential businesses shut down for a time. By March 23, 2020, life looked drastically different than it had two months before when we were cavorting around Disney World for a week of Pro Bowl fun. The kids were adapting to online education, and Dave was working remotely from our basement. We had decided to use our playoff bonus to do some work around our house that year. One of the pressing needs was to level up and plant grass in a large area in the backyard so it would be easier to mow, and thankfully, there would be less mud. We love working in the yard, and I knew I could be part of finding an easy solution.

As I walked by a huge mound of earth where two new homes were being built at the top of our hill, an idea popped into my head. I had a quick conversation with one of the men running the excavator, and 30 minutes later, they were dumping a load of dirt onto the tarp I had spread across our front lawn. Invigorated by my quick thinking and seeing the plan come together, I stood proudly watching. I knew this much dirt would have taken my husband at least four trips in his old truck. In the unknown of stay-at-home orders in the State of Washington, I felt like I had given us a chance to complete our project quickly and save money. There was just one problem.

Dave did not see it the same way.

The next morning, while I was inside supervising school and toddler play, Dave got started wheeling loads of dirt to the backyard. When I came out an hour later to check in, his frustration boiled over.

"This dirt was a terrible idea! There is way too much of it, it's full of rocks, and nothing is going to grow in it. It's all clay," he fumed.

I stopped, all of the energy in me draining away as I felt my defensive walls snap up like a steel cage around my heart. I stood still in the middle of our yard, the cool of early spring a stark contrast to the heat rising in my cheeks. I knew I had a choice for my next move: turn on my heels and flee or open up about the feelings of blame and shame that I was feeling. Drawing in a deep breath, I turned toward my husband.

"I wasn't trying to make more work for you. I was trying to help," I said, fighting to control my voice, anger and fear mingled in my response.

"I was just being honest." His reply wasn't sharp, but it stung just the same.

Another chance to be truthful. "Well, it really hurts my feelings!" I responded, this time turning away and marching inside. There was nothing more either of us could say at that moment. We both continued our work until I had a business question that needed an immediate answer.

———— ❖ ————

Dave: The second Lizzy walked away, I said to myself, "You idiot! She was just trying to help." I imagined Lizzy triumphantly walking down the street, guiding the dump truck to the tarp she laid down on our lawn to save the grass. I imagined the sense of pride she must have felt and the joyful anticipation of seeing my face when I thanked her for taking the initiative to get the dirt for free. It must have felt like she made herself vulnerable to me, and I betrayed her.

———— ❖ ————

Lizzy: I rounded the gate and found Dave adding another pile next to the row of mounds lining the backyard. He set the wheelbarrow down, walked straight to me, and gathered me into a hug. "I'm sorry I made you feel badly. I was feeling sorry for myself." In an instant, the walls between us dissolved, his humility and my faltering honesty creating space for us to reconnect.

He went on to explain that he was planning to use the rest of the dirt to fill in a huge hole in the ground our son had created from years of digging for buried treasure. We had recently lifted our shed as well, and the ground around it needed to be leveled. He pointed out the tally marks where he was keeping track of each wheelbarrow load. He led me to a growing pile of large rocks next to the original pile out front. "We can use these to finish the rock wall in your garden over here."

The best part of the resolution to this conflict came the next day when it was my turn to work on moving dirt. I was determined to make the second half disappear into the yard. I marked my tallies in a different color, each load creeping closer to the total he had marked the day before. I was bent on beating his number until I heard the gentle whisper in my mind, "Why did you want this dirt in the first place?"

To take work off my husband's plate and to help him to complete this project.

I kept the tally going, but now I was counting the total number together, the marks becoming a monument of the work we were doing *together*.

As I rounded out the second hour of digging, my back was really starting to hurt. Each shovel felt heavier and heavier, and I began to wonder if I was going to be physically capable of finishing the task. Just when I was getting ready to stop, Dave showed up with renewed energy and another shovel. For the next 30 minutes we worked side by side without exchanging a word. We were a whirling dervish, culminating with a team deadlift of one last giant load. It was the perfect amount. We rolled up the tarp, raked the rest of the rocks back into the garden, and put up the tools. Not 10 minutes after we finished, a torrential downpour started, tamping down all the new earth and washing away any evidence of the dirt in the front lawn. The tally marks disappeared, leaving no trace of the competition, just a freshly laid patch of dirt ready to grow something new.

We always have a choice. We can choose to stay in a world of self-protection and self-promotion, or we can put aside our pride and make our way toward each other. When we choose our own comfort and insist on being right, we remain two people separated and alone to fend for ourselves. The much harder decision is to engage with our conflict, each of us doing our own work alongside each other, until we come to a solution for our team. This is where the gold is. This is where we find our way into something truly beautiful in our marriage.

# CHAPTER 22

# THE TRAILHEAD

SEATTLE IS SO MUCH MORE THAN GRAY SKIES, the Space Needle, Pike Place Market, and lots of rain. To adventurers like us, it is an emerald-green wonderland of ocean wildlife, mountain trails, rivers, and lakes. There is no shortage of beauty. We can practically step outside our front door and be inspired. This is the backdrop for many of the lessons we have learned along this journey toward a thriving marriage. This stunning wilderness is also the greatest metaphor for the life we were called to together.

When we shared our struggles with Aunt Molly and Uncle Tom, they invited us to go on a hike called Sleeping Beauty, in the Mt. Adams wilderness area. This trail is well off the beaten path, and you'll likely not encounter another person on your pursuit of the summit. Rising before the sun, coffee mugs in hand, we left the comfort of the morning fire to hit the trail. The last five miles of the drive are on a gravel Forest Service road. By the time we finally reach the trailhead, the light of dawn filtering softly through the dense forest, we had already traveled 45 minutes from home.

The chilly morning air wrapped around us, the only sound the reverberations of the slamming car doors and hiking boots crunching in the gravel. The trailhead was a small wooden marker, one you would miss if you didn't know to look for it. The trail itself was a simple well-worn pathway between two trees, disappearing into the evergreen forest. Tom and Molly led the way into the woods. The idyllic beauty of the undisturbed wild soon gave way to labored breathing as we wound our way up the steep incline. The trees thinned the longer we hiked. At one point we had a brief respite as the trail leveled out and we traipsed on through the quiet woods.

When we came out of the tree line, we were met with the final obstacle. The last push to the summit was a quarter mile up steep, rugged boulders carefully crafted to form a narrow stairway up the ridgeline. The path was narrow, switching back and forth to the top. When we finally reached the top, we were staggered by the view: 360 degrees of sun-drenched alpine beauty, surrounded by Mt. Adams, Mt. Hood, Mt. St. Helens, and the many smaller peaks between.

We were thankful to be with them, honored that they would share one of their favorite places with us. It felt incredibly sacred. We sat down on a large flat rock top together, breathing deep the fresh mountain air and relishing in the astounding scenery. Tom pulled a Tupperware container from his backpack with hard-boiled eggs, baby oranges, and some nuts for us to share. As we ate gratefully, Molly asked an intriguing question.

"So, guys, if life is a trail, where would you say you are right now?" she asked in her characteristically thoughtful and intentional way.

"I feel like I've finally found the trailhead, and I have no idea what to expect next. But I'm ready to go find out," Dave answered honestly, an understanding of why they invited us to the trail slowly wrapping us in the warm embrace of further gratitude.

"That's good." She didn't offer any anecdotes or advice; she and Tom just sat there with us in our excitement and uncertainty, staring out over the basin. Being together in the slowly warming morning, at the top of this beautiful ridge, we were awash in hope.

Tom pointed off into the horizon and said, "See that kind of jagged-looking ridgeline off to the north there? That is Goat Rocks Wilderness. I used to get dropped off on one end and arrange for someone to pick me up a few days later on the other end of it. You should do it sometime."

We lit up at the thought of a new adventure. "We should do it together—the four of us. That would be so fun!" The thought of finding a new peak to climb was invigorating, and we were excited to get back down the trail to start preparing for it. This hike was the start of a quest for more mountain tops. Mailbox Peak, Tenerife Falls, and the Old Laurel Logging Road are just a few of the summits we completed, and just the beginning of seeking out new vistas. Sitting atop the ridgeline of another crest, drinking coffee from a Swell bottle, fueled our desire to always seek the next journey, the next challenge.

When you really think about hiking, it's pretty amazing how we travel so far and physically exert ourselves just to get to the peak and enjoy the view for only a few moments. After catching our breath for a little while, getting our legs back, we'll start looking for another mystical peak on the horizon together. When we find one that looks difficult enough to try, without saying anything, we'll share a look of exhilaration that says, "That one is next." The work is never finished. Your marriage will never reach a place where you don't have to head out again into unfamiliar territory.

It is our hope that by reading the truth of what this process has looked like for us, you will find the courage to find your next trailhead. Your journey will look different than ours, but there are guideposts that will help on the way.

- One or both of you will have to decide that what you've done up until now isn't enough.
- You'll have to commit to doing your own work, regardless of what your partner chooses to do.
- You'll be exposed, it'll bring up pain you wanted to forget about, and you'll probably want to run like hell more often than not. We promise that will get easier the more you practice.
- You'll need people around you who have been where you want to go (and those who are trying to go that way, too).

- You'll need professional help. We highly recommend finding a counselor. The scariest part of counseling for us was making the decision to go, and it has been nothing but an incredible gift since we've gone.
- Many experts and highly trained people have taken the time to put their knowledge into books. Please become familiar with the list of resources in the back of this book. These books have changed the way we see each other and relate to one another. Knowledge is an invaluable road map for you.
- You will need lots of prayer and likely a lot of coffee.

You were called to this moment. You were called to see this marriage as far as you both are willing to go. You don't have to wonder if your spouse is the right person. If you choose to become the right person yourself, your marriage has a chance. If you are both committed to doing this sacred work, you cannot even begin to imagine the heights you will reach. As an aside, we are not inviting you to stay in a situation that is not safe. This is not something God would ever ask you to do.

But for today, you need only one thing. You need to know that wherever this journey takes you, no matter the outcome, you will not be alone. God is right there with you. He didn't reveal himself to Elijah in the gale or the earthquake or even the fire, but in the quiet whisper when the chaos had passed. Elijah didn't have to find God because He was already right there, so close He barely had to speak. God is right here, asking you to take His hand and step out into the darkness—somewhere you have never been before. Now is your chance at the life you were made for... *together*.

# ABOUT THE AUTHORS

Dave Canales' coaching adventure started as a young boy, drawing plays in the schoolyard with his friends. Those experiences led him on a coaching journey from high school to an assistant coach on the staff of the Super Bowl champion Seattle Seahawks. Dave frequently invests his off-the-field time sharing his experiences regarding culture and leadership to organizations worldwide. When Dave is not coaching or consulting, you will find him having coffee with his wife Lizzy, fishing and playing with his four children, or giving the occasional haircut to anyone in need. *This Marriage* is Dave's first book and displays his life of powerful authenticity.

Lizzy Canales is a fiercely loyal friend, truth-teller, and silver linings expert. A mother of four, she spends her days cooking healthy meals, finding adventures to keep things fun, managing relationship dynamics, and being a sounding board for her husband's dreams—while still finding a way to throw around heavy weights or go for a run. A self-proclaimed recovering sorrow avoider, she discovered the magnificent, transformative love of Christ amidst her deepest pain. Through the process of writing her first book, she has discovered her passion for storytelling as a way to help other people feel like they are not alone in facing their losses, opening the door to a life where they can truly thrive.

# BOOKS WE RECOMMEND

*The Power of a Praying Wife.* Stormie Omartan. Harvest House Publishers 2007, 2014.

*Love and War.* John & Stasi Eldridge. Doubleday. 2009.

*Wild at Heart.* John Eldridge. Thomas Nelson. 2001, 2010.

*Captivating.* John & Stasi Eldridge. Thomas Nelson. 2005, 2010.

*Fathered by God.* John Eldridge. Thomas Nelson. 2009.

*The Road Back to You.* Ian Cron & Suzanne Stabile. Intervarsity Press. 2016.

*The Enneagram.* Andreas Ebert & Richard Rohr. Crossroads Publishing 2001, 2017.

*Healing Your Marriage When Trust Is Broken.* Cindy Beall. Harvest House Publishers. 2011.

*How We Love.* Milan & Kay Yerkovich. Waterbrook Press. 2006.

*How We Love Our Kids.* Milan & Kay Yerkovich. Waterbrook Press. 2011.

*The Brain That Changes Itself.* Norman Doidge, MD. Penguin Books. 2007.

*Reconnect.* Steve D. Call, PhD. Self-Published. 2019.

*You and Me Forever.* Francis & Lisa Chan. Claire Love Publishing. 2014.

*Love & Sex.* Nancy Houston. Regnery Publishing. 2018.

*It Didn't Start with You.* Mark Wolynn. Penguin Books. 2017.